BOOK+Art

Handcrafting Artists' Books

Dorothy Simpson Krause

NORTH LIGHT BOOKS

Cincinnati, Ohio
www.mycraftivity.com

13 12 11 10 09   5 4 3 2 1

Distributed in Canada by Fraser Direct
100 Armstrong Avenue
Georgetown, ON, Canada L7G 5S4
Tel: (905) 877-4411

Distributed in the U.K. and Europe by David & Charles
Brunel House, Newton Abbot, Devon, TQ12 4PU, England
Tel: (+44) 1626 323200, Fax: (+44) 1626 323319
E-mail: postmaster@davidandcharles.co.uk

Distributed in Australia by Capricorn Link
P.O. Box 704, S. Windsor, NSW 2756 Australia
Tel: (02) 4577-3555

Library of Congress Cataloging-in-Publication Data

Krause, Dorothy Simpson.
  Book + art : handcrafting artists' books / Dorothy Simpson Krause.
     p. cm.
  Includes index.
  ISBN-13: 978-1-60061-154-4 (pbk. : alk. paper)
  ISBN-10: 1-60061-154-0 (pbk. : alk. paper)
  1. Bookbinding--Handbooks, manuals, etc. 2. Books--Format. 3. Artists' books. I. Title. II. Title: Book plus art. III. Title: Book art.
  Z271.K755 2009
  686.3--dc22
                                    2008050258

Editor: Tonia Davenport
Designer: Corrie Schaffeld
Production Coordinator: Greg Nock
Photographer: Mary Taylor

fwmedia
fwmedia.com

FOREWORD

Artists have an enviable reaction to paper, ink, stone, thread and images, making works of art that I still would like to label "bookworks." At the outset, I always say that every artist has an innate desire to make a book. It involves sequencing, craftsmanship, finesse, but most of all it reflects content and context. No book should just be "beautiful." It should say something. It should mean something. And it should cast a wide circle.

I envision that future libraries will contain the very essence of artist books, where a streak of nostalgia will bring viewers and readers into the "rare book library" to see what artists have been doing for centuries, making bookworks that genuinely move the spirit, capture the imagination, and impart visual and verbal information that changes one's mind about many things and concepts.

In *Book + Art*, artists are challenged to focus on meaningful content and to extend the definition of book from the physical to the virtual—to create those unique objects we will treasure for posterity.

Judith A. Hoffberg
1934–2009
Editor and Publisher of *Umbrella*

ACKNOWLEDGMENTS

Although formally trained as a painter, I gained my knowledge of the book arts through workshops, sharing information and techniques with colleagues, research, reading, and trial and error. Through the years, I have worked with a number of book artists whose contributions I greatly appreciate. They include: Tim Ely, Shanna Leino, Bob Ebendorf, Laura Wait, Wendy Hale Davis, Keith Smith, Scott McCarney, Julia Miller, Peter Madden, James Reid-Cunningham, Marcia Ciro, Stephanie Stigliano, Sharon McCartney, Karen Gorst, Maureen Cummins, Suzanne Moore, Don Glaister, Janine Wong, Theresa Airey, Danny Conant, Sing Hanson, Catherine Steinman, Esther Maschio, Ana Cordiero, Katherine McCanless Ruffin and Mary Taylor.

Colleagues who have read the drafts of this manuscript and made invaluable suggestions for changes include: Sharon McCartney, Janine Wong, Mary McCarthy, Viola Käumlen, Bonny Lhotka and Karin Schminke.

Tonia Davenport, North Light's craft acquisition editor, encouraged me to undertake this book and made valuable organizational suggestions. Corrie Schaffeld is responsible for the understated, classic design.

I am especially indebted to my husband, Richard, for his continuing support and encouragement, and to my studio manager, Mary Taylor, an artist and teacher, whose insights and assistance are invaluable components in the creative process.

Dorothy Simpson Krause, 2009

Sicily, 2008, 56 pages, Images collaged in Sicily into a pre-made blank book (see pages 114–115)

CONTENTS

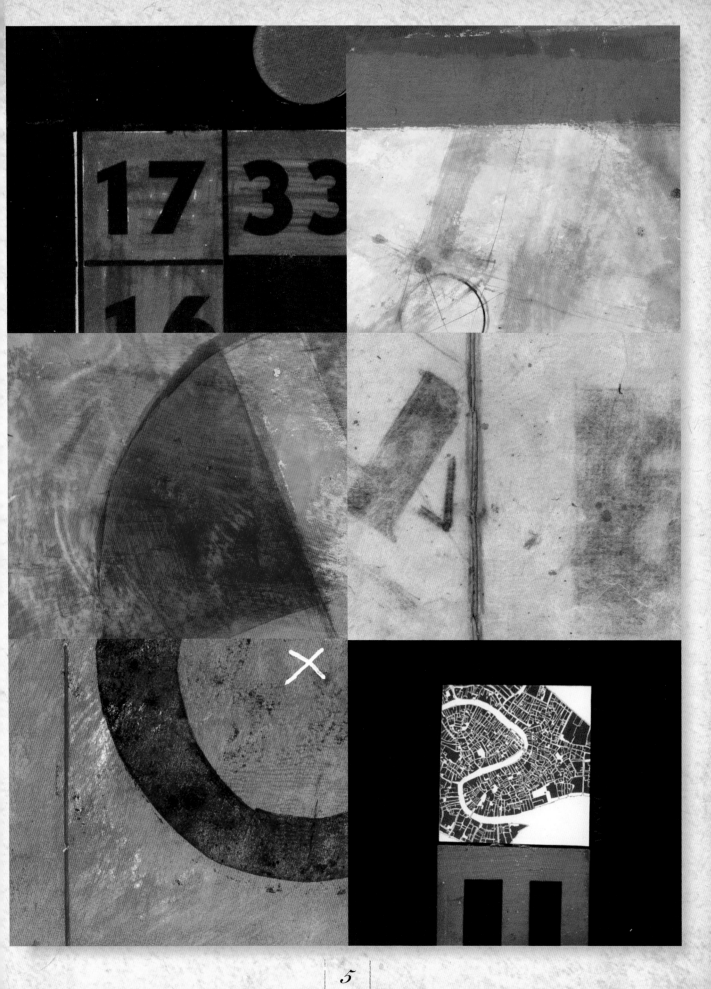

A Format for Artistic Expression

Some of our museums' greatest treasures are early books—hieroglyphics on papyrus, illuminated manuscripts on vellum and oriental scrolls on silk—presenting content with images and words. Beginning in the late 1800s, presses brought together artists and writers and published their collaborations in elegant editions. In the 1960s and 1970s, that tradition expanded to define books by artists as unique works of art. Today, hundreds of colleges, universities and art centers offer book-arts programs. Interest in book arts continues to grow largely due to the fact that it can encompass virtually any other art form, providing the opportunity to create added meaning in an intimate structure.

While some books may have an artist, writer, editor, designer, papermaker, typographer, printer and binder involved in the production, in artist books, the artist often does it all. And that's what you will be doing in this book. You will explore a variety of books and book-like forms, and learn processes and techniques that will allow you to make books as an expression of your art. For the most part, these unique books will be one-of-a-kind.

My involvement with making books began in 1998 on a trip to Vietnam. The blank journal I purchased had pages that were glued into a deep spine and a paper cover that wrapped around and closed with a strip of bamboo. Before I left home, I glued an irregularly shaped envelope inside the front cover. The structure allowed extra pages to be slipped within the deep spine and the envelope held scraps of cloth, gold-washed joss paper, medals and other found ephemera, until I incorporated them into the book.

When I returned, I scanned the pages of the journal into the computer, combined them with photographs, printed them on film and transferred them to handmade paper. The journal served both as a work of art in its own right and as a source of imagery for this series of unique digital monoprints.

A painter by training and collage-maker by nature, my primary focus has been large-scale work combining traditional and digital media. My early books allowed me to explore repetition and variation in a small format, and they provided a welcome escape from trouble-shooting computer problems. As books have become an increasingly important part of my work, I have focused on learning traditional book-making processes and adapting them to meet my needs as an artist. I have also begun to incorporate digital processes where appropriate and useful.

This book is designed to share what I have learned and to give you relatively simple and elegant ways of presenting your concepts and ideas. Demonstrations will present the processes, and Tips will give you additional information. Creative Explorations will challenge you to consider other options and will provide alternative insights. If you encounter a term that's new to you, look for its definition in the Glossary, and use the Resources section to locate the people, places and things I may mention.

Vietnam Journal, 1998, 54 pages,
6³/₈" × 6¹/₂" (16cm × 17cm) collaged journal

Vietnam Journal inside cover and Bananas for Breakfast, 1998, 22" × 30" (56cm × 76cm) digital transfer

What Is an Artist Book?

We generally think of books as those things that sit on bookshelves with pages, covers, words and images. But books may vary considerably from that description. A book can be loosely defined as an original work of art that provides links and meeting points between art disciplines in a book-like format. Although a book can be enormous or tiny and made from almost any material imaginable, most are made to be held, opened and closed, and, perhaps, viewed in a sequential manner. Most are intimate, requiring a degree of attention and contemplation to experience the condensed emotion or observation they contain.

What makes a book interesting is the relationship between the content and form, and how it functions to entice and engage. Although I began my involvement with making books by purchasing plain blank books that could be personalized, I now prefer to make my own. It allows me to choose the size, paper (or other surface), binding style and cover material that will work together to enhance the concepts presented by the images and words—concepts chosen from subject matter ranging from the personal to the political, the sacred to the mundane.

In *Book + Art*, we'll be referring to the individual parts of a book—covers, endpapers, book block and so on. We'll look at the basics—surfaces, images and words. Then we'll look at altering pre-made books and a variety of ways to make simple and elegant book structures to house your images and words.

Because this book is, of necessity and by design, limited in scope, you may want to explore particular threads in depth. One of the best sources of information on educational opportunities, professional organizations, tutorials, reference materials and galleries is The Book Arts Web www.philobiblon.com. Maintained since 1994 by Peter Verheyen, it is also the home of Book_Arts-L, an active electronic meeting place, and The Bonefolder, an e-journal for the bookbinder and artist. Look in the Resources section at the back of this book for other suggestions.

Inspiration and Perspiration

Thomas Edison's quote, "Success is ten percent inspiration and ninety percent perspiration," is significant in that he lists inspiration first. It is the impetus to create that drives the creative process, and while inspiration can come from many sources, if we always waited for a brilliant idea to emerge, we would probably do little work. It is usually in the process of working—the perspiration—that we find the inspiration.

As you search for inspiration, consider taking a workshop, going to a place you think would be of interest, applying to be an artist-in-residence or putting together a group of artists with similar interests who can be a productive support group. Many artists find they need an exhibition deadline to spur their productivity. All of these options put you in situations where you can explore ideas while working.

Do whatever you can to give yourself the time to work. Don't wait for inspiration to strike. Start looking for visual or narrative components that relate to an issue of importance to you. Think about the message you want your work to communicate and how you can communicate it simply and effectively.

Tools and Materials

While being able to work uninterruptedly is ideal, for most people, it is an unrealistic expectation. If you can find a space where your work can be left in process, it will be much easier to return to it whenever you can, even if only for a brief period. If you have to put your things away at the end of each session, set up a system that will allow you to start, stop and clean up as quickly as possible to give you maximum working time. Clear plastic bags and boxes make organization easier and allow you to see through them to find what you need.

Tools and materials are integral to every step of the process, and there is considerable overlap in those used for making art and making books. Although the following list is long, few of the items are absolutely necessary and will vary according to the way you choose to work. If you are a fiber artist, you may choose to work with fabrics and trims, and use machine or hand sewing. If you are a printmaker, your etchings, etching plates and inks may become your materials of choice. Whatever your media, you certainly won't include *all* of the materials and tools listed.

While most of these supplies are found in art stores, my favorite shopping places are yard sales, flea markets, recycle centers, dumps and secondhand stores. In used bookshops, you can find wonderful old books to alter, as well as book covers, illustrations, text pages, letters, maps, documents, photos, postcards and stamps. In hardware stores, there is nonwoven fabric, wire, screening, aluminum, lead, copper and wood. Craft and fabric stores have fabric, interfacing, lace, thread, twine, wire, raffia, yarn, string, ribbon, buttons, beads, wood and tin shapes, and wooden and papier-mâché boxes.

In the following lists, feel free to substitute wherever possible. General information is given here, and specifics are discussed in the various chapters. Items or brands are occasionally suggested by name. Usually there are acceptable substitutes, but if there is no alternative for an item, it is noted.

Artmaking

Since the books you make may incorporate your art as well as being art objects in their own right, you should begin with the art materials and tools you normally use and add other media as they seem to expand what you are trying to accomplish.

Basic

Apron

Chopping mat, thin and lightweight hard surface

Craft sticks

Gloves

Mixing bowls, measuring cups, spoons

Pans

Paper and other substrates for making art and books

Paper or polypropylene bags or sheeting to cover work surface

Paper towels

Paper, scrap for gluing—newsprint, old phone book or catalog

Pushpins

Sponge, large household

Spoon, spatula

Staple gun, heavy-duty staples

Dry Media

Pastels, oil pastels

Pencils, graphite, colored, water-soluble

Pigments

Wax crayons, water-soluble crayons

Wet Media

Acrylic paints

Alcohol

Blender

Brushes, a variety of sizes 1/2" (13mm) to 4" (10cm) for paint, paste and glue, bristle, foam, toothbrush, roller, cotton swabs

Faux finishes, crackle glaze, rust

Ink, acrylic, pearlescent, metallic, black, walnut

Oil paints

Pens, metal nibs, markers, gel, metallic

Turpentine or substitute

Watercolor, gouache

Printmaking

Brayer, 4" (10cm) or 6" (15cm) soft rubber
Collagraph plates
Cutting and carving tools
Gelatin, Knox unflavored
Inkpad
Palette for inking, nonabsorbent
Printing inks, water-soluble
Rubber stamps, commercial, wine corks, erasers, soft rubber, craft foam with adhesive back
Stencils

Encaustic

Cheap bristle brushes
Cold wax medium
Cold wax metallic pigment, like Rub 'n Buff
Encaustic medium (beeswax and resin)
Heat surface for encaustic: small crock pot, electric fry pan, metal bowl or can on small warming tray
Hot air or heat gun
Tacking iron or household iron

Mediums, Texturing Materials, Precoats and Postcoats

Acrylic mediums, liquid or gel, gloss, satin, matte
Calcium carbonate, whiting or athletic field marker
Gesso, white and black
Inkjet precoats, like Golden Digital Grounds
Modeling (or molding) paste
Spackling compound
Spreaders, credit cards or pieces of plastic
Varnish or postcoat, like Golden Gel Topcoat or Krylon Crystal Clear

Transfer Materials

Acrylic gel medium (hand sanitizer, like Purell)
Citra-solv
Clear packing tape or contact paper
Transfer film, like DASS
Lazertran, inkjet or silk
Rub-on letters
Safe-release masking tape

Bookmaking

There are many pieces of equipment that bookbinders use to make life easier, but for the artist who makes one-of-a-kind books, the investment in money and studio space makes finding alternatives or work-arounds a reasonable option. For example, a substitute for a press can be improvised with a board on each side of the book and spring clamps or a weight on top. The tasks done by a guillotine or board shear for trimming the edges of books or cutting bookbinder's board can be accomplished with many thin cuts of a sharp snap-blade knife. These techniques and many others are discussed at various points throughout the book.

Basic

Awl or needle punch
Board, binder's, book, mat, wood
Brush, paste and glue
Calipers
Chopping mat, thin, lightweight, hard surface
Clamps, spring or similar, clips, paperclips
Cloth, leather or paper for pages and covers
Cutting mat, self-healing, large and small
Dental floss threader, like Eez-Thru
Eraser, white and black, like Factis
Folder, bone or Teflon
Knife, snap-blade, X-Acto (craft), heavy utility or scalpel with extra blades
Microspatula
Mull, muslin or long-grained rice paper
Needle-nose pliers
Needles
Pencil and sharpener
Pickup, natural rubber
Piercing cradle
Rubber bands
Rulers, metal, preferably with cork back
Sanding block, fine
Scissors, large, small like Easy Kut mini
Screw punch or paper drill
Straightedge
Strips of wood, plastic or metal
T-square, long, metal
Thread, linen or other strong, cord
Triangle, metal, 90° and 45°, 6" (15cm)
Tweezers
Wax or substitute, like Thread Heaven
Waxed paper
Weights, small

Adhesives

Several adhesives are useful in making books. For the most part, I use acrylic gel medium because it is thick and introduces little moisture. If more saturation or a longer drying time is needed, PVA or a mixture of PVA and wheat paste works well. I find double-stick tape and adhesive laminate especially useful, and I like the portability of glue sticks when traveling. The properties of some adhesives are discussed below. Whenever possible, choose brands that claim to be archival.

- Polyvinyl acetate (PVA) glue is one of the most common adhesives. It is a thick, sticky and fast-drying white glue. PVA may be mixed with wheat paste or methyl cellulose to give it additional working time. Jade and Sobo are high-quality and readily available brands.
- Methyl cellulose, a plant-based starch, is prepared by adding water to it.
- Acrylic mediums are good as adhesives (and also for inkjet transfers and surface texturing). Thicker gel mediums have the most binding properties and are least likely to migrate through papers and cause problems on the surface. All acrylic mediums are archival.
- Double-stick tape and adhesive laminate in clear sheets may be used to glue together any two surfaces, but they are especially useful to invisibly adhere two transparent surfaces like Plexiglas and clear film. Tapes, like 3M Scotch 969 or 924, are referred to as "adhesive transfer" tapes. They are designed for use in an applicator but can also be applied by hand. MACtac manufactures crystal-clear sheets of adhesive film for mounting. As with all laminates, they are best applied under pressure. Gaffer's tape, a matte black version of duct tape, is often useful.
- Glue sticks, paste in a solid form, are great for traveling. They are neat and quick drying, and they won't cause paper to wrinkle, but the quality from one brand to another varies considerably.
- Craft adhesive is a clear compound that bonds to wood, metal, fabric, leather, glass, ceramic and found objects. Clear Liquid Nails and E-6000 are readily available brands. UGlu makes an industrial-strength bonding adhesive in strips.
- Spray adhesive is tempting to use, but it may release over time and may also turn brown and migrate through the paper since most are not pH neutral. To avoid messy overspray, spray into a box or outdoors.

- Hide glues are a traditional component in paper sizing, canvas preparation and the making of fresco surfaces. Rabbit-skin glue crystals are probably the most common.
- Wheat paste, commonly referred to as "paste," may be made from a variety of products, with precipitated wheat starch or rice starch being the preferred products of many bookbinders. The recipe included below is generalized and can be adapted easily.

If you are not careful, glue or paste can leave unwanted marks on your book. Place a clean sheet of scrap paper under your work each time you glue. Pages from a phone book or catalog work well.

Recipes for Wheat Paste

Cooked

Mix 3 tablespoons white wheat flour with just enough cold water to make it wet and liquid enough to pour. Bring to a boil 1 cup of water. Pour the cold wheat flour mixture slowly into the hot water, stirring constantly. Bring to a boil. Cook while stirring until thick. Allow the paste to cool before using. Store in refrigerator.

Precooked

Talas wheat paste is a precooked powder that dissolves in cold water with hand beating or a blender. It requires no heat source and is quick to make. Sprinkle ¼ cup precooked wheat paste into 1 cup of water. Blend until all lumps are smooth and the mixture is the consistency of heavy cream. If you prefer a slightly thicker mixture (the texture of pudding), that you can draw or write into, add an additional 1 tablespoon of wheat paste. Store in refrigerator.

Digital

Although most of my bookmaking is done with traditional media, I also use a digital camera, scanner, computer, inkjet printer and Adobe Photoshop. Since these are becoming more common tools in artist studios, some of the demonstrations show how I use them in making books. If you don't have a computer in your studio, there are other ways to accomplish many of these techniques.

In choosing a printer, it is helpful to have pigment inks for longevity (see Permanence below), a straight paper path to accommodate rigid materials and as much head clearance as possible. Some desktop printers can print on materials 1/16" (1.5mm) thick, which will allow you to texture or collage surfaces before printing.

Most desktop inkjet printers have ejection rollers or "pizza wheels" that come in contact with the image immediately after it is printed. This creates no problem on a porous medium like paper, but if you want to print on a nonporous surface like metal or film for transferring, the ejection rollers may track or drag on the surface and damage the print. The mechanism holding the "pizza wheels" can be raised or "shimmed" on some desktop printers, and the wheels can be removed on others. Search on the Web to see what artists have found applicable for your printer. The printer used in these demonstrations is an Epson Stylus Pro 3800, a 17" (43cm) wide printer that meets all of the criteria listed above. In 2004, I co-authored *Digital Art Studio: Techniques for Combining Inkjet Printing with Traditional Art Materials* with Karin Schminke and Bonny Lhotka. It contains additional information you may find of interest.

Permanence

The terms "permanent" and "archival" lack agreed-upon definitions. They generally refer to the stability or resistance of a material to changes over an extended period of time. While we all want our work to last as long as possible, there are intriguing ways of working and interesting items to be found almost everywhere—and there is no substitute for the patina acquired with age. Your choice of materials may affect the life of your artwork, especially if you are a mixed-media artist using found collage materials such as newspaper clippings and rusty metal.

With the advent of pigmented inks, the fading of inkjet prints is no longer the problem it once was, and in books that are largely closed and the images protected from light, dye inks should also work well. Wilhelm Imaging Research, Inc. conducts accelerated aging tests, primarily for printer and ink manufacturers, to determine the comparative life expectancy of inkjet and other digitally printed images with various inkset and paper combinations and posts the results on their Web site. Golden Artist Colors is an excellent resource for technical and conservation information on acrylic paints, grounds, mediums and specialty products.

Safety

While all of the processes described in this book, if used as directed, present no known health hazards, it is always good to take proper precautions and follow instructions related to the materials you choose to use. Material Safety Data Sheets (MSDS), which list the ingredients and any warnings about use, are available from most manufacturers. If you find you are bothered by the fumes from some products, use them sparingly or outdoors. Pay close attention to the directions for safely using encaustic and polymer clay, and carefully monitor the maximum temperatures at which they are heated. If you have concerns about a particular product, request information. Art Materials Information and Education Network (AMIEN) provides information regarding the quality, durability and health hazards of artist materials.

Some processes use household tools. One example is using a blender to make smooth wheat paste. Although in this case there would be no harm in reusing the blender for cooking, as the wheat paste is edible, it is a good idea to segregate all studio tools to avoid potential health problems. And, as a precaution, keep your materials closed and away from food, children and animals.

Copyright

Copyright is designed to protect original expression from unauthorized use. It begins at the time the work is created in fixed, tangible form. In most cases, the artist who created the work holds the copyright. A work that is no longer copyright protected is considered to be "in the public domain" and can be used without permission or payment. If you incorporate images, words or objects that may be under copyright, and you anticipate that your work will be shown, sold or published, you will need to determine how to best proceed. Web sites related to copyright issues are linked through The Book Arts Web. Whenever you use other people's works, give them appropriate credit in the text, a footnote or the colophon.

Colophon

A colophon is a note, usually located at the end of a book, giving publication details. It may list the papers and typefaces used, date of completion and number of copies printed, and, in the case of a limited edition, it will cite the copy number. It also may identify the author, artist, designer, illustrator, printer and publisher. While not a necessity, a colophon is a nice addition to a handcrafted book.

What's Next

In the first section of this book, we'll explore paper and other substrates, images and words. Then we'll work with pre-made blank books and altering existing books. Next, we'll make a variety of handmade book structures based on folded sheets, adhesive and sewn structures. Finally, we'll consider covers, boxes and unbound collections.

There are endless variations on everything covered in this book. Feel free to adapt any of the processes to meet your talents and your needs. And, most of all, just enjoy creating!

Scrap of Cloth, 1998, 22" × 30" (56cm × 76cm)

Helpful Hints

- Use the art and book tools and materials you have, substituting where possible.

- Cover your work surfaces with plastic bags, plastic sheeting, paper or chopping mats to make clean-up simple. I have 4' × 8' (1m × 2m) sheets of polypropylene, a plastic nothing sticks to, on my work tables.

- Check with a framer or commercial printer to see if you can get scraps of mat board or papers trimmed from their projects. Pieces that are too small for them to use are often perfect for book pages and covers, and large quantities can be had for little or no cost. A woodworker may be a good source of interesting woods.

- A craftsman who works with leather, making handbags or clothing, may also have scraps large enough for spines, separate front and back covers, inlays and onlays. Although you will probably have to pay a nominal charge, it will be much less than if you were buying skins, and you will have a variety of colors and textures. Clothing leather is thin and soft and, it doesn't require paring to wrap around boards.

- A weight, which can act as a substitute for a book press, can be made from a flat-bottomed pan filled with bricks.

- Spring clamps can also act as a substitute book press. Be sure to put your book between rigid boards so that the clamps won't leave marks.

- A small weight, especially useful for holding your book open when sewing, can be made by covering a brick, buckshot or other heavy item with fabric, or by using a piece of metal or polished stone scrap. If you can find one, an antique flat iron is both functional and aesthetically pleasing.

- A bone folder will make marks on paper and fabric; a Teflon folder is more expensive but leaves no marks. You can clean a bone folder by sanding, but sanding a Teflon folder releases particles that are hazardous to your health.

- A can nailed or screwed to the edge of your worktable is a handy and safe place for a hot air gun.

- A piercing cradle, used to make even holes for sewing, can be simply made from binder's board (see page 102).

- Some of the supplies I find most useful are:

  Double-stick tape, when traveling or where moisture from paste or glue would create a problem.

  A black eraser doesn't mark on black paper and seems to also erase what other erasers don't.

  A natural rubber pickup lifts glue smears.

  Mini spring-action scissors are small and sharp, and they can be carried aboard planes.

  Calipers allow me to measure and make divisions without dealing with numbers.

  A microspatula is great for making sharp folds and applying paste in tight spaces.

  Chopping mats are inexpensive, thin and lightweight, and they provide an easily cleaned, reusable, hard surface between book pages for rubbing a transfer or keeping dampness from migrating to adjacent pages.

Travel Supplies

When I travel, I carry a 9" × 12" (23cm × 31cm) clear expandable plastic envelope that holds my book and a few sheets of papers I think may be useful. I also have a pencil case that contains a limited selection of pencils and felt-tip markers, small tubes of watercolor or gouache, a brush, a Teflon folder, mini spring-action scissors, a ruler, an eraser, a pencil sharpener, rubber bands, double-stick tape and glue sticks. The scissors, which resemble tweezers, have never been questioned by airline security. If I think I will need them, I also carry a snap-blade knife and a small self-healing cutting mat in my suitcase. Along the way, I gather collage materials that are added to my envelope and used in creating the book pages. Most of my travel journals are created with this limited selection. The selection shown was used in the creation of Land of the Inca and Sol.

SURFACES, IMAGES AND WORDS

Although a book may not have all three of the basic components, it would, at the very least, have a surface. And the surface would most likely contain images, words or both—the book's content. The most common surfaces are paper, in all its variety, but many other substrates are possible. We'll begin by exploring surfaces that you can use for pages and for covers, including synthetics and unusual options. Then we'll consider ways of working with images and words, and look at how the components work together.

Nag Hammadi, 2006, 72 pages 5" × 3¹⁄₂" (13cm × 9cm)
Nag Hammadi is a single quire made of sheets of mud papyrus. The brown leather cover is attached to a single signature with two black leather tackets. A tie of the same brown leather is attached to the cover with three visible stitches of black leather and a tail left hanging. The black leather is also used to make ties at the head and tail of the wrapped cover to secure the book when it is closed.

Paper and Other Surfaces

Although many materials can be ordered online or from a catalog, there is no substitute for feeling a sheet of paper when deciding which one to choose for a project. Fine-art papers, printmaking papers and papers made for the offset and laser markets may have different nomenclature, but in all cases, the characteristics of paper include the:

- weight—expressed in grams per square meter (gsm) in the fine-arts world and in pounds (lb.) for the offset/laser market—with the lowest numbers for very lightweight and the highest for papers heavy enough to stand alone

- surface/texture, which may be decorative, as with embossed papers, or utilitarian, as with watercolor or pastels papers, whose textures are designed to hold the media

- opacity, which ranges from see-through sheer to completely opaque

- process by which it is made—handmade, mouldmade or machine-made

- material(s) from which it is made, with options including banana bark, mulberry papyrus, cotton and synthetics

- sizing—the way a paper is coated—ranging from heavy sizing in watercolor papers to an absence of sizing to increase absorbency, like a waterleafed blotter paper

- thickness or caliper, often measured in millimeters (mm)

- brightness or whiteness, sometimes expressed as a number from 1 to 100, with the higher number being the brightest

- color, which may be subtle or neon bright, made from natural or synthetic dyes, and be fugitive or colorfast

- optimization for various media, including watercolor, pastel, printmaking and digital

- acidity or pH factor, with acid free or a pH factor of neutral (7 or slightly greater) being preferable

- wet strength, referring to the ability to hold together and not dissolve when wet

Some of the papers that work well as the underlying substrate for both making art and making books include drawing and printmaking papers and, if you are printing from a computer, digital "fine art" papers. Smooth hot press papers like Arches Cover (white and black),

Hahnemühle Biblio or Schiller, Rives BFK, Moab and Fabriano Roma are some book artist favorites. They stand up to layering multiple applications of media. Lighter weight papers, like Canson Mi-Teintes, are good for working with collage and dry media. Very sheer, lightweight oriental papers can be used with drawing media when a delicate surface is appropriate or collaged onto other surfaces. There are also very opaque papers that are precoated on both sides, designed for inkjet printing of books.

Using colored, decorated, textured, patterned or preprinted papers can give your book a head start and provide an additional interest to the surface. In planning a book to take on a trip to Santa Fe, I chose a variety of rough textured papers in beige and turquoise, the color of sand and sky, and a complementary acrylic paste paper. Collage, graphite, colored pencil and copper foil were used in this book, exploring the settling of the West.

West, 2005, 24 pages, 7½" × 6¾" (19cm × 17cm)

Grain

Paper grain is the direction in which most of the fibers of machine-made paper lie, due to the motion of the machine during manufacture. Handmade and mouldmade papers have less apparent grain direction, or none at all. Paper tears more easily with the grain than against the grain, and, for some types of paper, folds made parallel to the grain will cause less damage to the

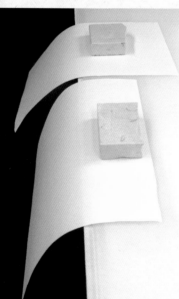

paper and will be less bulky. When paper is moistened, the fibers expand more across the grain, so when pasting together two surfaces, the grain of both should be aligned to prevent one from expanding more than the other, thus preventing wrinkles. In books, the grain of every page should be parallel to the spine.

One of the best ways of determining the direction of the

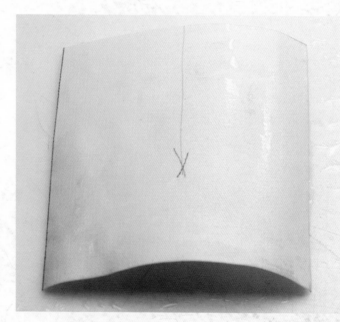

paper grain is by placing two pieces of the same paper, one oriented horizontally and one vertically, on the edge of a table so that approximately 6" (15cm) hangs over the edge. The direction that shows the greatest droop has the grain aligned with the table edge. If this isn't clear, another more destructive method for determining the direction of paper grain is to cut a 2" (5cm) square of paper, marking the orientation of the paper from which it was cut. Lay it flat, and wet one side with a wet sponge or paper towel. The paper will curl with the valley of the curl in the grain direction since most of the expansion is cross-grain. Other methods I've found less useful include: holding the paper by one corner and spraying the opposite corner—it will curl with the grain; bending the paper vertically and horizontally—the "springier" direction is against the grain; and tearing the paper in each direction—the straighter edge is with the grain.

When paper is listed by the dealer, the second number is supposed to be the long grain. So 22" × 30" (56cm × 76cm) indicates that the grain on the 30" (76cm) direction is long. Some dealers use an underline for the dimension to indicate the grain direction. Since this is not universally practiced, it is usually good to check for yourself.

Deckles

Sheets of handmade paper will have four natural, irregular edges, referred to as deckles, which are created in the papermaking process. Mouldmade papers usually have two actual deckle edges and two torn or cut edges. You can create the handmade effect of a deckle edge by careful tearing. Although some bookmakers feel that deckle edges are used to cover poor skills, I find them appealing and incorporate one or more deckle edges wherever appropriate.

Synthetics and Other Options

Most papers made from natural fibers will warp and wrinkle when glue or wet media penetrates the surface. Some papers, films and fabrics made of synthetic materials are dimensionally stable (they won't buckle, swell or shrink). Although they are very different in texture and weight, Strathmore Aquarius II watercolor paper, Sheer Heaven, Yupo, Dura-Lar and nonwoven fabrics made with spunbonded polyester, polyethylene and polypropylenethe are all dimensionally stable synthetic products.

Leather, vellum, cloth, acetate, Plexiglas, metal, metal foils, wood, wood veneer, glass, aluminum, clay and polymer clay are possible materials that can be used in making pages and book covers.

For inkjet printing, virtually anything that will go through your printer can be coated with an inkjet precoat. (See the sidebar on page 20.)

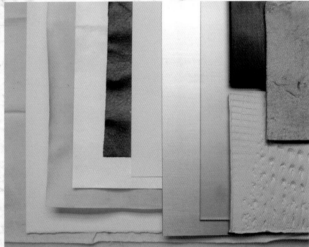

Synthetics and other options: muslin, Aquarius II, vellum, Tyvek, leather, Yupo, aluminum, Plexiglas, wood, clay, polymer clay

Texture may be given to a synthetic surface with acrylic molding paste (a heavier form of acrylic gel medium) or other materials and tools.

Some of the wide range of substrates you can use are shown below and throughout the remainder of this book. Be aware of the possibilities, and consider using interesting surfaces in inventive ways.

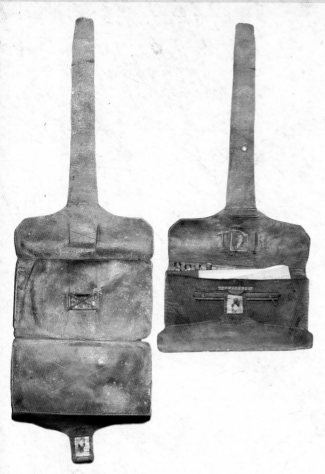

Folio, 2001, 5" × 7" × 2" (13cm × 18cm × 5cm) closed
Made from a handmade antique leather folio that a farmer or traveler might have used at the turn of the century. The inside pockets were used to house bits of ephemera relating to that time.

Negative Memory, 2006, 4 pages, 5" × 7" (13cm × 18cm) closed
Glass "pages" wrapped in copper foil with heavy tape hinges became Negative Memory. A positive image from one of the negatives was transferred to patinaed copper foil for the cover. The foil was nailed around the edges of wood and a small cross and rub-on letters were added.

Entombed, 2001, 7" × 7" × 1½" (18cm × 18cm × 4cm)
Made from an antique lead box with encaustic coated images from Pompeii.

Altering the Surface

Surfaces can be altered for practical and for expressive effects. Processes may be applied under the image and words, or they may be applied on top of all or part of the image and words. These processes may be transparent, translucent or opaque. Single or multiple pages can be cut, torn or folded for edge effects, to make room for collaged materials or to create openings from one page to another. Sewing, abrading, punching holes and embossing will also create surface effects, as will the addition of texturing materials such as encaustic, molding paste, pumice, gesso, sand, calcium carbonate and powdered marble dust. A clear crackle glaze wiped with burnt umber acrylic so that paint is left in the cracks will age surfaces like primed canvas and painted wood.

You can change the surface of Plexiglas, clear film or other plastics by sanding, which will also provide a roughness to which acrylic paint can adhere. Both sides of the sheet can be painted to yield dimensional qualities, or other materials can be placed behind to show through. Sanding leather can also create interesting dimensionality.

The subliminal quality of the page surfaces, including the edges and the backs of the pages, unused but visible, are frequently underestimated, and therefore underutilized.

Pieced Together, 2002, 10 pages, in a tin box 6¼" × 4¾" × 2¼" (16cm × 12cm × 6cm)
A concertina book, with collaged paper quilt blocks and text from early documents, was made in the Amish country near Lancaster, Pennsylvania, and housed in a box found on the trip. To further reference a sewn quilt, Pieced Together has stitching-like patterns made with a large needle. When open, light passes through the small holes in the collaged pages. Encaustic was used to tie texture the collaged surface.

Inkjet Precoats

Inkjet precoats are products designed to coat substrates prior to inkjet printing. These precoats allow you to print on any porous/absorbent or nonporous/nonabsorbent surface that will go through your printer. Plastics and metals should be cleaned with alcohol or diluted vinegar then washed in hot water before precoating. If you have "pizza wheels" (see Digital on page 11), the clear precoats may show track marks on nonporous surfaces, but matte white will create an absorbent surface that the wheels won't mark. Iridescent precoats are available, or metallic pigment may be added to clear precoats to create interesting effects.

Flattening Paper

Moisture from media or glue may cause your paper to curl after it has been painted, textured or precoated. Try one or more of the following methods for flattening the paper:

- While still damp, hang it from one corner and let it continue drying.
- Roll it in a loose roll in the direction opposite the curl.
- Place it under a heavy board overnight.
- Put it through an etching press or cold laminator.

If you have wrinkles in paper that has dried, protect the paper surface with a silicon sheet and use an iron or a heat press to introduce warmth and pressure.

Aging Paper

If it is appropriate for your book, giving paper an appearance of age can be very effective. Different papers will give very different results, and variation from page to page can be visually advantageous.

In the fall of 2006 I found a small tile of the ship Mayflower while in Moravian Pottery & Tile Works in Doylestown, Pennsylvania. I had Nathaniel Philbrick's book *Mayflower* with me on the trip, and I thought it was an interesting coincidence, so I bought the tile. As I read, I was struck by Philbrick's accounts of the slavery of Native Americans. When I returned home, I downloaded maps of New England in the early 1600s, spent a day photographing the replica of the Mayflower, visited Plimoth Plantation and bought several parchment facsimile documents in their gift shop. Aged papers seemed an appropriate possibility on which to print the photographs.

Materials

Paper to age

Water

Strong solution of black tea or coffee

Walnut, brown or black ink

Instant coffee granules, walnut ink crystals or salt

Inexpensive bristle brush or toothbrush

Sponge or paper towels

Optional: inkjet precoat

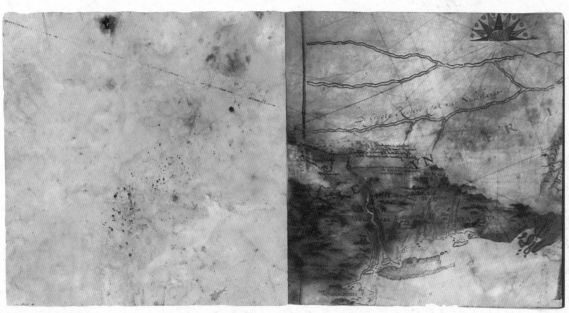

Aged pages overprinted for Mayflower, 2008

1. Wet the surface of the paper and add black tea, coffee or diluted ink, allowing the color to flow irregularly. Shake on instant coffee granules or walnut ink crystals to add dark spots, and salt to irregularly absorb the water. Use a brush to feather out some of the darker color, and a sponge or paper towel to soften and blot the surface. Crumple the wet paper to create cracks. If both sides of the book pages will be seen, also work on the back of the paper.

2. An alternative to using darkening stains to age documents, is to wash them with white. Here, instead of using paint, I mixed white matte inkjet precoat with clear precoat to make it translucent and give the paper a surface for inkjet printing.

Images

If you're like me, the content for a book typically veers heavily on the image side and may be suggested by a series of photographs, paintings, collages or found objects. You may be inspired by a book, a movie, an article or an event, and over a period of time, you acquire imagery that reflects this inspiration. A single image per page is rarely adequate to convey the complexity of a concept, so I usually layer images, or images and words, using both traditional and digital media applications.

There are three characteristics that seem to recur in my work, regardless of my chosen imagery: reflectivity, a patina of age and a color palette in shades of black, brown, red and gold. I have always been drawn to brown paper bags, faded photographs, oxidized metal, crumbling walls, peeling paint, raveling fabric, foxed paper, antique mirrors, stained leather and other worn surfaces. Think about what elements are most favorable to you, and try to incorporate these components into your work whenever you can.

There are many ways of incorporating images into your book, including collage and a range of printmaking, painting and drawing techniques. Under the generic term "mixed media," you can cross the boundaries, combining and layering the processes into an unlimited number of possibilities. Let's look at the basics first.

Magdalene Laundries, 2003, 72 pages, 6 × 4½" (15cm × 11cm) collage in leather coptic binding over papyrus (see the cover on page 119)

Collage

The term *collage* is derived from the French "coller," meaning "to glue." It usually refers to a work of art created by pasting bits of ephemera—photographs, cloth and small objects—to a flat surface. With the advent of scanners, digital cameras and computers, the possibilities for combining diverse elements has exponentially increased. You can preserve the original components while changing their scale, color and transparency, then print them as individual pieces or combine them in the computer to create digital collages. Your components and collages can be printed onto a range of diverse media for layering or transferring.

Most of my books made while traveling are collaged from materials collected on the journey. I was in Ireland when Peter Mullan's movie *The Magdalene Sisters* was released. It told the true story of the unmarked graves of 133 women, discovered in 1993 when one of the laundries held by the Sisters of Charity in Dublin was to be sold. Over the 150-year history of the laundries, 30,000 women were held in servitude. That shameful history became the impetus for the book *Magdalene Laundries.* The cover is shown on on page 119.

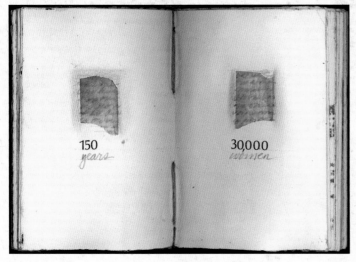

"150 Years" from Magdalene Laundries

"Penitent" from Magdalene Laundries

Printmaking

In printmaking, ink is transferred from a prepared surface to a receiver surface, usually paper. Some of the simple printmaking supplies and processes that can be used without a press are stamps, block prints, collagraphs, stencils and monoprints (including digital transfers).

The terms *monoprint* and *monotype* are often used interchangeably, but a monotype can't be repeated, and a monoprint has at least part of the image on a fixed surface that is potentially repeatable. For simplicity, we are using the term *monoprint* for both of these transfer processes.

To make a monoprint, ink is painted or rolled onto a surface such as film, Plexiglas or gelatin. Paper is placed against the inked surface, and the image is transferred through absorption or pressure by hand rubbing, burnishing or rolling with a brayer or rolling pin. The process permits only one print, though if ink remains on the plate, a very faint, or "ghost," print may also be made.

Stamps

Stamps (which are not always rubber) can be purchased, or carved from wine bottle corks, erasers or soft rubber sheets, using your own drawings. Stamps are generally pressed against ink pads, which vary tremendously in quality and composition, then pressed against the paper onto which the image is transferred.

Block prints—cut from rubber, linoleum or wood—may be printed either with ink rolled on the surface of the block or with ink forced into the areas that have been cut away and the surface wiped clean. Old etching plates may also make interesting prints.

Embossing powder, especially used clear over clear ink, is an effective and subtle touch to provide dimensionality.

Collagraphs

Collagraphs are dimensional collages composed from a wide variety of materials—including cardboard, spackling compound, thin foam sheets and textured materials—that are inked and printed. They may be simple and used alone, or combined with other collagraphs and image-making techniques into a complex image.

Stencils

A stencil is a template made by removing sections from paper, cardboard or acetate to create the negative form of an image or text. Pigment is applied through the removed sections, leaving a reproduction of the stencil on the underlying surface.

Signs and Symbols, 2006, 40 pages, 10½" × 5½" (27cm × 14cm)
collagraph prints, stencils and stamps over acrylic paste paint

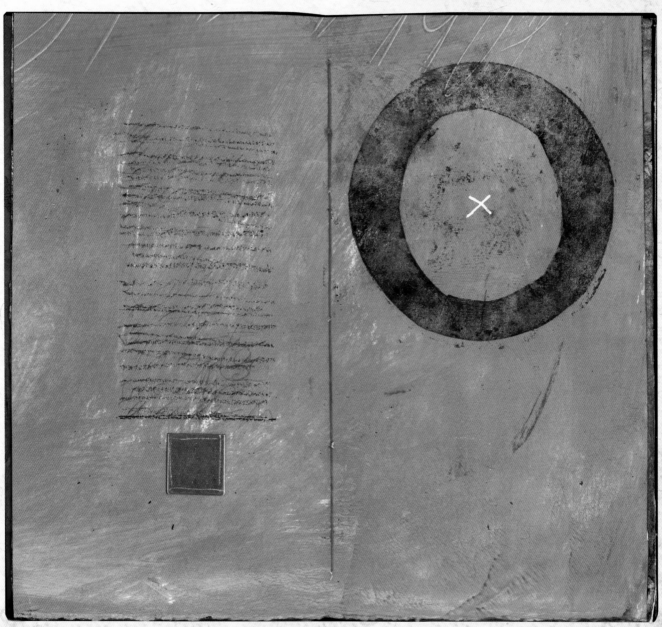

Painting and Drawing

Watercolor, acrylic and oil paints each have very different properties. Traditionally, watercolor uses transparent, water-soluble pigments mixed with a binder, such as gum arabic, that is washed onto relatively rough-surfaced, absorbent paper. Acrylic paints may also be thinned with water, but use synthetic resin as the binder, which forms a tough, flexible film that is impervious to water when dry. Oil paints hold the pigments in a binder like linseed oil. It dries much more slowly than watercolor or acrylic and must be cleaned with turpentine or other spirit. The paper, canvas or board, which serve as the substrate, should be sealed with acrylic to prevent the oil from penetrating and damaging the surface.

There are other variations of paint, including water-mixable oils, gouache (a heavy-bodied opaque watercolor), egg tempera (a very quick-drying paint using egg yolk as a binder), casein (a paint using milk as a binder) and encaustic (pigment in beeswax).

Drawing is usually thought to be the making of marks on a two-dimensional surface where line is more dominant than mass. It may be a sketch, plan, diagram or model created to develop an idea in another medium, or it may be a finished work of art. Drawings can be done with a wide range of tools, traditionally including pencil, charcoal, pen and brush. The difference between painting and drawing may lie only in the artist's definition of his or her own creation.

Common Ground, 2008, 60 pages, 7³/₄" × 6" (20cm × 15cm)

Common Ground focuses on the land that we hold in common—sanctuaries, preserves and protected areas. It includes prints, paintings and drawings on a variety of papers, including Mylar and a heavy black handmade paper with embedded gold threads. It has a painted and laser-engraved wood cover and leather spine sewn over tapes shown on pages 116-117.

Encaustic

Encaustic, a medium made from beeswax with resin added to harden and stabilize the wax, is both a painting medium and an interesting way to texture surfaces. Melted over low heat and applied thickly, it is milky and can be ironed smooth or textured with brush strokes or tools. Applied thinly, it can be fused into the paper with an iron or hot air gun to create a translucent surface. Mixed with pigment, it can

be applied like paint. Before working with encaustic, research the many ways in which it can be used. Do not exceed the recommended temperatures for melting wax, handle hot tools with care and be sure to have adequate ventilation.

A microcrystalline cold wax medium is available commercially from manufacturers like Dorland and Renaissance. Rub 'n Buff is a similar product with metallic pigment. You can make your own cold wax medium by putting beeswax shavings or wax pastilles into a jar, covering them with mineral spirits or turpentine and allowing it to sit overnight. Cold wax medium is especially useful over media that might smear or transfer to another surface since it functions as a sealer.

Encaustic can be used over any other media, but only oil paint can be used over encaustic. Use inexpensive brushes and dedicate them for use with wax.

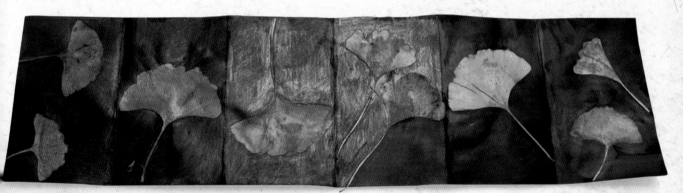

Ginkgo, 2004, 6 pages, 7" × 5" (18cm × 13cm) closed, concertina on Arches black cover with ginkgo leaves, encaustic, gold leaf, silver leaf, pigments and graphite

Mixed Media

By combining traditional art materials with digital printmaking techniques, you can create unique work that takes advantage of the best of each process. You can begin by printing a digital image, then adding collaged elements or virtually any traditional art media, including paint, pastel and colored pencil. This is a great way to produce a series of images with a number of variations created by treating each print in a different manner. Translucent, metallic and interference paints are especially interesting over digital prints.

You can also reverse the process by beginning with a painting, collage or piece of printed material that can be put through the inkjet printer to add a digital layer. Since inkjet inks are translucent when printed, they are a good way of adding overlays that integrate underlying imagery.

Some of the most interesting works use traditional media in nontraditional ways—for example, making acrylic paste paint by combining acrylic paint and wheat paste to make a thick, smooth, semi-transparent paint that can be marked and written into. Applying whatever paint you choose with sticks, rags or airbrush is another example.

In the following demonstration, we'll be making paintings that we will scan and combine, in the computer, with photographs. The digital files will be printed on top of the original painted pages.

Overprinting Acrylic Paste Paintings

Materials

Paper, large sheet, approximately 22" × 30" (56cm × 76cm)

Wheat paste (see recipe on page 10)

Acrylic paints

Brushes

Craft stick

Folder

Aluminum ruler or straightedge

Optional:
digital files of images, scanner, computer, imaging software, printer, white paper for carrier sheet if needed

Acrylic paste paint, a mixture of acrylic paint and wheat paste, is quick to make and keeps in the refrigerator for several days. You can vary the opacity by changing the paint-to-paste ratio; the more paint there is, the more opaque the color will be. You can also make the paint thicker by using less water in the wheat paste. By painting on a large sheet of paper then cutting or tearing it into smaller sizes, you can create interesting and unexpected compositions on the resulting pieces. Use of the computer in Steps 3 and 4 is optional. You can also overprint with one of the other printmaking processes if desired.

Consider the size of the paper, its grain and how you can maximize the number of pages with the spine of the book parallel to the grain. (See pages 17–18 for more information on paper grain.) In this project, a 22" × 30" (56cm × 76cm) sheet was torn into two 22" × 15" (56cm × 38cm) pieces, then four 11" × 15" (28cm × 38cm) pieces. Finally, it was torn into eight 7½" × 11" (19cm × 28cm) pieces and folded to eight 7½" × 5½" (19cm × 14cm) folios.

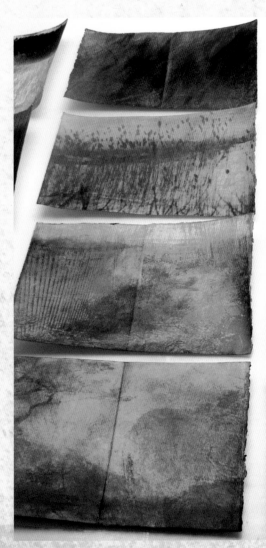
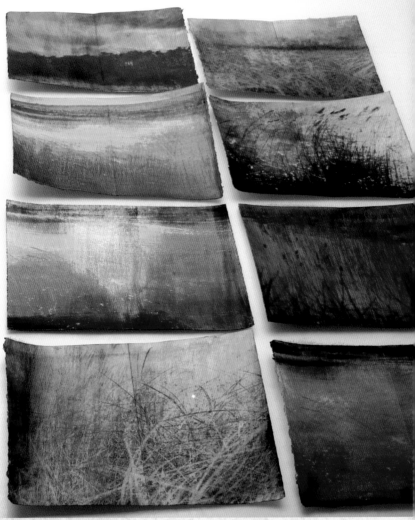

Inkjet prints over acrylic paste painting

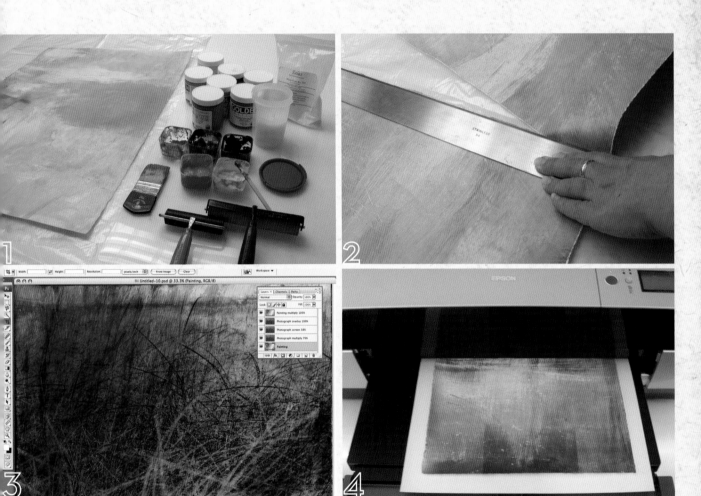

1. Mix a small amount of wheat paste with a small amount of acrylic paint. Paint the acrylic paste paint over the entire sheet of paper. Draw, write or texture into the thick surface of the paste paint. Let the sheets dry thoroughly.

2. Fold the sheet in half, along the grain, and smooth the fold with a folder. Using an aluminum ruler or straightedge as a guide along the fold, cut or carefully pull the paper at a 45° angle. Fold and tear those two pieces into two pieces each, and then fold and tear those four pieces into two pieces each.

3. Scan the painted pages into Photoshop or a similar photo-editing program, and choose photographs or other images to combine with them. Work with layers and the various adjustment options to create unusual combinations. Size your image file to print (bleed) over the deckle edges. As a final step, turn off the layer with the scanned, printed page, so that it won't print.

4. Print onto the painted pages. Overcome the problem some printers have with seeing deckle, painted or clear edges by placing your painted page on a larger sheet of white paper, leaving a margin on the leading edge and the side for the printer to read and print. Fold the prints into double-page spreads (folios) and tone the raw, torn edges with paint if you like.

Gelatin Monoprints

Materials

Pan for making gelatin plate
(smooth-bottomed if you are unmolding)

Mixing bowl (or mix in pan)

Measuring cup

Spoon or spatula for stirring

Mixed gelatin to fill your pan
to a level of at least 1" (3cm)

Refrigerator

Piece of newspaper or other soft paper

Optional: flexible chopping mat
(or similar) for unmolding gelatin plate

Papers, smooth

Materials for texturing or printing

Water-soluble block printing ink

Soft rubber brayer

Palette for inking brayer (chopping mat or
other nonabsorbent hard surface)

The process described here was originally developed by Fran Merritt, founding director of the Haystack Mountain School of Crafts, and then refined by Sharon McCartney. With this method, water-soluble printing ink is worked onto the surface of a "plate" of firm gelatin. This is a quick and easy way to make a print; you just need to plan ahead since the gelatin needs several hours to become solid.

The gelatin plate may be left in the pan or unmolded. Unmolding the plate allows you to use a larger paper size than the size of your plate and creates an interesting edge pattern. Without the support of a pan, a thicker block is easier to handle.

Gelatin Recipe

The basic recipe is 2 envelopes Knox Unflavored Gelatin per 1 cup water. For a 6-cup pan, use 12 envelopes gelatin and 6 cups water—three hot and three cold.

Gelatin Prints in Copper, 2000, 88 pages, 8½" × 7¼" (22cm × 18cm) mixed-media collage with gelatin prints

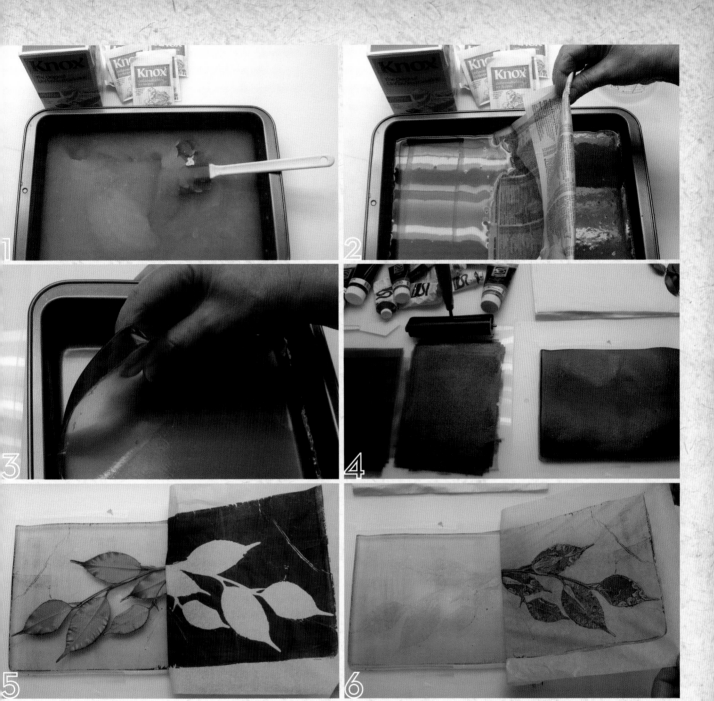

1. Decide on the amount of gelatin needed for your pan and adjust the recipe. If the gelatin is to be left in the pan, the block can be ½" (13mm) thick. If it's being unmolded, the block should be ¾"–1" (20mm–25mm) thick for easier handling. Place the pan on a level surface and add the cold water. Sprinkle the gelatin over the water in the pan. Let the gelatin swell until it looks like applesauce. Add the hot water and stir gently to completely dissolve the gelatin.

2. Gently drag a piece of newspaper or other soft paper across the surface of the gelatin to remove any bubbles.

3. Leave the gelatin on the table until it begins to gel, then move the pan to the refrigerator for several hours until the gelatin is solid. Remove the gelatin from the pan, if desired. Separate the edges of the gelatin from the pan edges by pulling with fingertips. Unmold the block by placing a chopping mat across the top of the pan and turning it over. Allow the gelatin block to stand at least an hour at room temperature to dry out a bit.

4. Place the ink onto a palette, and spread it by rolling with a brayer. When the brayer is evenly coated, roll the ink onto the gelatin plate. The coating of ink should be slightly transparent over the gelatin. Too much ink will create a blurry, watery print.

5. To make a negative print, lightly press objects onto the surface of the inked gelatin. Lightly press smooth paper over the objects. Burnish firmly, rubbing by hand. (You are only pressing into the ink and not the gelatin, so be gentle.) Remove the negative print.

6. To make a positive print, following the negative print, carefully remove the objects from the gelatin plate. Ink will remain where the objects were. Place paper onto the gelatin plate to pick up this remaining ink. Burnish firmly, rubbing briskly (but still gently) by hand. Remove the positive print.

Inkjet Transfers

Materials

Paper,
smooth printmaking

Inkjet print of a
horizontally flipped image
on DASS Transfer Film

Alcohol gel
hand sanitizer, like Purell

Spreader, credit card,
piece of plastic,
foam brush or brayer

Rubber brayer

Folder

There are four components in the transferring of inkjet-printed images from one surface to another: the film on which the image is printed for transferring, the printer and ink, the transfer medium, and the paper or receiving surface onto which the image is transferred.

All inkjet transfer film has a pre-coat that allows the water-based inkjet dyes or pigments to adhere to its surface. (See Inkjet Precoats on page 20.) While most precoats on these films are designed to hold the ink stably, by chance, a few films have a precoat that allows the ink to be released when it comes in contact with a transfer medium. The medium creates a bond to a receiving surface stronger than the precoat bond to the film, and the ink is moved to the receiving surface.

Designed especially for inkjet transfers, DASS Transfer Film is available in both rolls and 8½" × 14" (22 cm × 36cm) sheets. It's clear so placement is easy, it prints on desktop printers without "pizza wheel" tracking and it transfers with a wide range of mediums, including alcohol gel.

I have tried many transfer mediums, including water, methyl cellulose, wheat paste, gelatin, various acrylic mediums and alcohol. None compare to alcohol gel hand sanitizer, like Purell. The use of this product for making transfers was discovered by Bonny Lhotka and demonstrated in her DVD. If you're transferring into a bound book, alcohol gel introduces very little moisture and dries quickly with little or no wrinkling of the paper. A smooth printmaking paper makes the best receiver.

Inkjet transfers may also be called digital monoprints. They have an irregularity, depth and character not found in straight inkjet prints, and they are a simple way of incorporating photographic or other digital imagery into books.

Images should be flipped horizontally before printing so that when they are transferred, facedown, they are correctly oriented; this step is especially important with text.

Helpful Hints

- If you are transferring inkjet prints into a bound book, place a flexible chopping mat beneath the receiver page to provide a hard surface for burnishing.

- If you are printing on unbound sheets and have access to a press, you can soak your receiver paper in water, blot and put it through a press to transfer the image under pressure or use a waterleaf paper like Arches 88 and transfer by hand.

- If you are printing on a transparency film and track marks appear, you need to address the problem of "pizza wheels." (See page 11)

- Purell alcohol gel hand sanitizer can be found in grocery and drug stores. Other brands may have different levels of effectiveness as transfer mediums.

- Some transfer artists mist their printed film with isopropyl alcohol in a spray bottle. It is a hazardous substance if inhaled and should be used with extreme care.

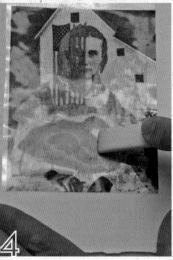

1. Evenly spread alcohol gel on smooth paper. You should be able to see the gel on the paper but have none standing on the surface.

2. Place the printed film facedown on the coated paper and roll with a brayer, or smooth with your hand, to remove air bubbles.

3. Wait one minute, then lift a corner to check the process of the transfer.

4. Carefully replace the film and rub with a folder to move any parts not transferred completely.

5. Remove the film and let the transfer dry thoroughly. The image used in this project is "Independence Day," one of a series of twelve large mixed-media pieces inspired by a group of poems about the family of one of the early settlers of the Plymouth Colony, "Macomber House," by Ray Amorosi.

Creative *Explorations*

- To add another dimension to your transfers, draw onto your transfer film using colored pencil, marker, crayon or oil stick. You can work on top of inkjet prints or on unprinted or scrap film. Remember, if you add written text, it will transfer in reverse.

- Before transferring your inkjet print, use water to "move" the ink, or sandpaper to abrade the surface and give it texture.

- Explore some of the many other transfer techniques discussed on the Internet.

- Toner-based transfers from a photocopier also have potential. One process for transferring text is discussed in Words. (See pages 38–39)

- Acrylic gel medium is also shown being used for transferring text to acrylic paint in Words. (See page 39)

- Inkjet prints onto Lazertran waterslide decals work well for many projects. One is shown in Unbound Collections. (See pages 134–135)

- If you are interested in further exploring nontoxic printmaking, look into polymer and polyester plate printing.

WORDS

Along with images, the other elements that can carry a book's content are words. In many books, text is the primary vehicle for conveying the message; there may be no images, or they may simply illustrate the text. Conversely, in many artist books, images may carry the message, and there may be little or no text. Where there is a combination of text and image, the ways in which they may be combined are infinite.

In this section, we look at what you are trying to say with your words, and how you are saying it visually. Your words may be something you compose or something you find, including phrases, essays, narratives, stories or poems.

Words may take your reader on an external or internal journey, record your dreams and aspirations, provide healing and insight, serve as a confessional or a chronicle for future generations or be a catalyst for creative expression. You may use techniques like free-association, automatic writing or list making. What you choose to say will, in most cases, determine how you choose to say it.

Because what I'm trying to say is frequently being defined in the process of making the book, my words are often incorporated in a fragmented, broken style using different typefaces, sizes and methods of application, including found text, writing, transfers, stencils, rubber stamps and computer prints. In Vietnam, I bought a rubber-stamp alphabet, taped together into a small rectangle with the letters out of order and upside down, and a red stamp pad. The alphabet has become a recurring motif in many of my books, symbolizing for me our difficulties in understanding one another.

Copper, 2000, 88 pages, 8¹/₂" × 7¹/₄" (22cm × 18cm) mixed-media collage

This was a handwritten, collaged journal that recorded whatever I chose to incorporate into it during the course of a year. It included the inane and the insignificant and wasn't intended for others to view or read. On the pages shown, my writing follows the lines of suminagashi marbling on brown kraft paper torn from a bag, while the opposite page incorporates a "perishable" rubber stamp, bottle label and fragment of corrugated cardboard.

Nag Hammadi, 2006, 72 pages, 5" × 3" (13cm × 8cm) acrylic paste paint, collagraph prints and collage on mud papyrus

The text in this piece came from a narrative poem in one of the thirteen single quire codices, or manuscripts, dating from the fourth century, found in 1945 near the Egyptian town of Nag Hammadi, buried in an earthen jar. It was an appropriate text since the book was a quarter-scale replica of one of the manuscripts. Written in the voice of a woman, it seeks to unite opposites. Throughout the book, I've combined imagery with passages from the text, written and printed in black, white, gold and silver ink.

many truths 2004 2 pages 4³/₄" × 10¹/₂" × 5¹/₄" (12cm × 27cm × 13cm) wooden bookstand and metal book with printed paper inset coated with encaustic

The simple text used here references the multiplicity of religious beliefs in India, where the wooden bookstand and hinged metal "book" were both found. The inside of the metal was measured and, in Photoshop, fonts were used against a black background to appear as if the "one" in the original text, "one truth," had been roughly crossed out with red and "truth" made plural with the addition of the word "many" and an "s." The two pieces, printed on paper, were glued into the metal and coated with encaustic to tie them physically and visually to the book form.

Writing, Type and Found Text

Calligraphy often merges written word with image. But unless you have mastered this art form, varying your handwriting may be a preferable way of adding text. Consider elongating your cursive writing with extended connectors between letters, making each letter extremely tall or extremely small, or turning your paper so that you are writing on the vertical, the diagonal or around objects. You can vary the look of these techniques by your choice of writing implement. You can choose pencil, colored pencil, marker, pen or brush and ink or paint, ruling pen, pastel or crayon. Or improvise a tool from a quill, stick, piece of cardboard or whatever you think may work. Vary the size of the implement's tip and change colors—even within words—to create variety and special effects. You can fill the spaces around and within letters with color, or, if you are writing with wax crayon, you can paint over the letters to add color. You can also write into thick, wet surfaces like acrylic paste paint, gel medium or gesso, using a paint eraser, stick or other implement. Writing may also be incised into encaustic works.

Letterpress, a printing technique that transfers ink by pressing raised type onto paper, is the most elegant and distinctive way of putting text on a page, especially in the hands of a printer who loves type and is attuned to the nuances of leading and kerning. For those of us without access to a letterpress or acute sensitivities, there are alternatives that, depending on your aesthetic, may even be preferable. Rubber stamping, embossing, transferring, stenciling and using rub-on letters are some of the ways to add type. If your pages are unbound, the computer and printer are another alternative. There are thousands of computer fonts available online, ranging from elegant and classic to distressed and degraded to period-appropriate handwriting. Many are free or relatively inexpensive.

Found text can include virtually any words on virtually any surface, and it can be used as content or as a graphic element.

Labeling Women, 2005, 40 pages, 6" × 5" (15cm × 13cm) mixed-media collage covered with marbled paper and silk spine

Women from Roman art are glimpsed through window and door frames cut from a piece of decorative paper and "labeled," correctly and incorrectly, with terms used to refer to women, including sister, mother, mistress and dame.

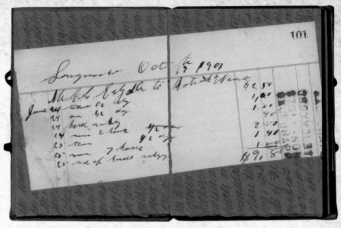

One Life, 2003, 43 pages, 5³/₄" × 4¹/₂" (15cm × 11cm) glass photographic plate on cloth keyhole binding, paper, collage

The book *One Life* began with a collection of turn-of-the-century letters and documents found at a flea market—all related to James Ward of Longmeadow, Massachusetts. Black and brown papers were chosen as backgrounds for the collaged pages. (See the cover on page 109.)

Cuba: History Rewritten, 2001, 53 pages, 6¹/₄" × 6¹/₄" (16cm × 16cm) mixed-media collage recovered in brown paper with expanded black cloth spine and hand fishing line

In Cuba, I found a history book published in Havana in 1925, prior to Castro. I began to focus on the differing perspectives authors bring to their accounts, and how time and political persuasion affect, counteract and obliterate viewpoints. The pages from this and other books and periodicals, Communist manifestoes, published letters, State Department brochures, poems and newspaper clippings became the primary components in my journal. This palimpsest—written, drawn, erased, crossed out and reworked repeatedly with remnants of erasures still visible—became *Cuba: History Rewritten*.

Creative Explorations

- Look at various placements of words and images on your pages. Consider how the size, shape and relationship between them affect your concept.

- Make writing implements from knitting needles, chopsticks, skewers and twigs.

- Consider unconventional materials for your writing, like roofing tar and amber shellac.

- Explore a form of "automatic" writing in which you write a stream-of-consciousness flow of words related to your content, combined with letter-like forms that don't make words but carry the flow.

- Make a collection of free and inexpensive fonts from online sources.

Transferring Text

Materials

Paper or book as receiver

Black-and-white fresh toner photocopy of horizontally flipped type

Citra-solv (a natural all-purpose cleaner found in hardware and health food stores)

Q-tips

Paper towels

Spray bottle

Safe-release masking tape or repositionable tape

Folder

Chopping mat or other nonabsorbent hard surface

Optional: digital files of images, scanner, computer, imaging software, printer, white paper for carrier sheet if needed

It's often useful to be able to transfer text into your books. If black text is adequate, this method, requiring only a copy machine and a solvent, provides a simple means.

If you want to carefully plan the placement of your text, scan the page into Photoshop and place the type in a separate layer over the scanned page to determine where it best fits. You can change the typeface, size and weight until you decide what is most satisfactory. When the layout of text on each page is complete, you can select the text and place it onto its own page, either alone or combined with groups of text. Then flip the text page horizontally (so it will read correctly after the transfer), print and photocopy with a toner copier. To emphasize some of the text in *Apologia* (see pages 50–51), I followed these steps.

Respectability: Its Rise and Remedy

The very first form of property was the ownership of women ❧ The Romans captured the Sabine women, because that was the regulation thing to do. Our pity need not be wasted upon the women—they simply exchanged owners—they were slaves in either case.

Males were not at first made slaves, because it was inconvenient—there was danger of uprisings; it caused discontent among the slave women, and for a man there was no market while a woman was in demand. She was valuable: first, as a wife, and second, as a worker. There are animals where the lordly male holds a dozen or more females captive, but it was man who first set his females at work ❧❧❧ Darwin says there is no doubt that marriage was at first a matter of coercion and purely a property right. Certain ceremonies even now go with the transfer of real estate and most other property, and the marriage ceremonial was, in the beginning, a public notification of ownership and a warning to all parties to keep hands off. The husband had the power of life or death over the wife and her children ❧❧ She, being a slave, performed all the menial tasks—she was the worker. And the product of

her labor belonged to her lord ❧ Thus we get the genesis of property:

First, the man owned the woman.

Second, he owned all that she produced ❧ The man produced nothing—he was the protector. To be sure, he killed animals, but he did not deign to skin them nor prepare the flesh for food—woman did all this ❧ For him to work would have been undignified and disgraceful—only slaves worked. And so to prove his prowess, his true greatness, he never did a thing but kill and consume.

Respectability: Its Rise and Remedy

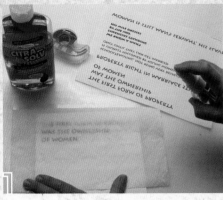 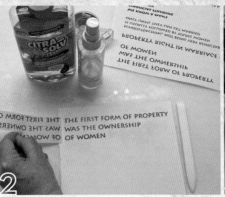 

1. When you have cut the text piece you want to transfer from the fresh toner copy, there are two ways to apply Citra-solv: you can dip a Q-tip into the solution, blot lightly on a paper tower and dampen the text area, or you can cover the text with a piece of paper towel and spritz it lightly.

2. Place a nonabsorbent surface, like a flexible chopping mat or silicone craft mat, under the page to protect the pages below from migrating solvent. Tape the dampened text on the appro-

priate page using a safe-release or repositionable tape. With a folder, burnish with heavy, even pressure in one direction. The transfer process is easy on some papers, like hot press, and is less perfect on other papers, such as those with a texture.

3. On paper that has texture, like the handmade paper in *Apologia*, transfers are a bit more unpredictable, but that imperfect look may be desired and is often appropriate, depending on your subject.

Helpful Hints

- Inkjet prints onto Lazertran waterslide decals work well on many surfaces. A transfer to a metal case is shown on pages 134-135.

- If you use waterslide decals to transfer text into your book, Citra-solv can be used to dissolve the decal edges, giving the appearance of integration with the surface.

- Text printed on sheer silk tissue can often be made to meld into the book page by coating with acrylic medium or encaustic.

- Rub-on or vinyl letters in a variety of fonts can be bought in sheets and easily transferred to other surfaces by rubbing gently. Since each letter is separate, you must align them carefully.

- Explore some of the many other inkjet transfer techniques discussed on the Internet. In one, the image is printed on paper, the surface of the image and the receiver sheet are coated with acrylic medium and the image is placed facedown on the receiver encapsulating the image between layers of medium and gluing the two sheets of paper together. To expose the image, the back of the carrier paper is wet and carefully removed by rubbing.

- Text from several pages can be combined onto one page for printing. Just be sure to flip the file horizontally before printing.

- Text printed with light colors or in a lightweight or small sized typeface may be difficult to read when transferred. Keep your choice of font relatively large, heavy and dark—it will be more legible and parts that break or don't transfer well will be less of a problem.

Two simple transfer techniques, which can be done with colored text, are inkjet-printed Lazertran waterslide decals (see pages 134-135) and gel-medium transfers.

Placing Text

Materials

Paper, sheet to be folded into double page spread

Text

Image

Pencil

Ruler

When deciding where to place your text on the page, you could use the same judgment you apply to other aesthetic elements and components, or follow a common contemporary convention that on each page the gutter and bottom margin will be slightly wider than the top and side margins. Or you could use an approximation of the golden section, a ratio found in medieval manuscripts. In this demonstration, we'll use the golden section to place text and, if you choose, to place images as well.

One of the classic page proportion guides for the placement of text is the Van de Graaf canon. The proportions vary with page size, but this adapted illustration works with book pages with a 2:3 ratio, such as 5" × 7½" (13cm × 19cm) (2½ × 2 = 5 and 2½ × 3 = 7½). The margins on the pages are proportional, 2:3:4:6 (inner:top:outer:bottom)—based on ¼" (6mm) increments. So the inside margin is ½" (13mm), the top margin ¾" (19mm), the outside margin 1" (25mm) and the bottom margin 1½" (38mm). The height of the text area is equal to the page width.

Because I'm primarily a visual person and have difficulty with mathematical ratios, I prefer to draw a diagram that works with all sizes and shapes of paper.

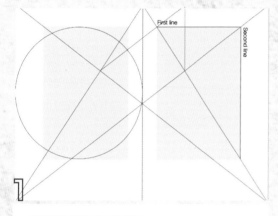

First line
Second line

1. Using this illustration, make a sample or fold your sheet of paper into two pages and lightly draw all of the black guidelines, except the circle. The first line defining your placement rectangle should be drawn parallel to the top edge from the V point on the upper right-hand page to the outer diagonal. Your second line will be parallel to the side edge until it reaches the next guideline. With these two lines, you can complete the placement of the golden section.

Autumn at Macomber House

In his own acre
a man bends to know
what of his seed;
with the back of a finger
he brushes the still
invisible hair of the world.

2. Select your text and, if you wish, an image. The image I've chosen, In His Own Acre, uses a scan from a handwritten draft of the poem "Autumn at Macomber House" by Ray Amorosi, a photograph of my grandfather and a photograph of marsh grasses. Place your text and image into the golden sections. As I placed my components, I realized that my text was too brief to occupy the space well, and that my image was considerably wider than these ideal proportions. (The area extending beyond the section is grayed out.)

Autumn at Macomber House

In his own acre
a man bends to know
what of his seed;
with the back of a finger
he brushes the still
invisible hair of the world.

3. Consider alternatives. I can use this layout if I crop my image to the proportions of the section or change the proportions to suit the image and text. Alternatively, I can cover the page with a larger cropped image and can use the right, left or both sections as guides for the placement of the text. I find this option less restrictive and more in keeping with my aesthetic choices.

Creative Explorations

- Explore various brands of water-soluble printmaking inks. The viscosity varies from brand to brand and even from color to color within brands. You can mix brands and also tone ink colors with tube watercolors or gouache.

- Use multiple colors of ink like paint and draw with tools into the surface of the ink, using brushes, feathers, stencils, rubber stamps or string.

- Experiment with a variety of papers and fabrics in different colors, textures and weights. Smooth papers and tightly woven fabrics tend to work best.

- Since light-colored printmaking inks are opaque, experiment with using them over dark papers or papers with patterns. Try white, silver and gold over inkjet prints.

- If you're not happy with a print, build up the surfaces. Use it as a layer and print on top of it with another ink color or another image.

- Cut a gelatin plate into shapes, separating them slightly to create interesting edges.

- Make a freeform gelatin plate by rolling a rope of clay and pressing it onto a glass sheet to form a complete frame or well. Pour the warm gelatin into the well and when it is solid, remove the clay rope. This alternative creates interesting edges and is easy to handle because you don't have to unmold the gelatin.

- Group together papers and other surfaces that may work for a particular concept you want to explore. Just the process of making material choices sometimes triggers new ideas. Consider including materials like corrugated cardboard, metal foil and wrapping paper. Some of the surfaces will work as pages, covers or collage materials and some can even be used for all three.

you know the
name of it´? Why
does she look
at it`?
What has she on her head`?
What has she in her ears`? Is
she a vain girl´?
If she is vain, is she good´?

BLANK BOOKS AND ALTERED BOOKS

From the wide range of commercially available blank books and journals, in this chapter, we will look at selecting a book and adding content with images and words.

We'll also look at altering an existing book. This approach gives you a ready-made starting point since the book will suggest the content and approach, and the pages already have images or words to which you can respond. With an altered book, we'll be looking at repetition, variation and sequencing.

Bennington, 2000, 100 pages, 8¼" × 5¼" (21cm · 13cm) pastel and pencil in purchased blank book with brown paper and corrugated cover.

Blank Books

A purchased blank book, which is plain enough for you to personalize and fill, is a good way to start. Since you have few structural decisions to make, you can focus on the content. If you want to work over a long period of time—for example, making a diary or sketchbook for the season or the year—choose a book that that has a sufficient number of pages to meet your needs. If you want to celebrate a visit or event of shorter duration, a thick book might be overwhelming, and one with fewer pages, or pages that can be removed, may be preferable.

There are many blank books available in book and stationery stores that are good choices. The size, shape, cover material, paper type and binding style are all considerations. For travel journals, I like a size similar to a postcard so that I can complete the pages with relatively small collage materials. I also prefer a wrapped binding style, like those used in *Promised Land* and *Planned Environment,* which allows for the inclusion of ephemera without stretching the book out of shape.

Promised Land, 2001, 32 pages, 6¹/₂" × 5" (17cm × 13cm) mixed-media collage in blank book
On September 11, 2001, when terrorists hijacked planes and flew into the World Trade Center and the Pentagon, I was in the Middle East trying to understand this territorial and religious conflict. I kept a collaged journal in a purchased blank book with a soft leather binding to which I glued a decorative found metal object. After the 11th, everything turned upside down, and the journal combined found materials with images from the world news.

ReViewing the Planned Environment, 2002, 76 pages, 5¹/₄" × 4¹/₂" (13cm × 11cm) mixed-media collage in blank book
While in Fort Myers, Florida, for an exhibition of my work at Florida Gulf Coast University, I found city-planning documents with environmentally impacting grid-like plans—which I contrasted with natural materials—handmade banana leaf paper on the front and back covers and a wood closure with hemp cord and clay ties.

India, 2004, 124 pages, 7¹/₄" × 4³/₄" (18cm × 12cm) mixed-media collage in blank book re-covered with unryu paper; found materials on cover and closing from India

During three weeks in India I kept a visual journal that incorporated ephemera collected during my travels to Bombay, Jaipur, Agra, Delhi, Chennai and Goa. The journal was so distended by the collage materials that when I returned, it had to be rebound. I also found the components for three other books, *Guardians* (see page 69), *many truths* (see page 35) and *law and custom* (see page 101).

Helpful Hints

- If you are using a wet medium like watercolor or acrylic, be sure to choose a book with heavy paper; otherwise, the pages may wrinkle badly.

- If you plan to add collage materials into your book, be sure the binding will accommodate the thickness of the added materials. A soft, wrapped leather binding with a tie that can expand is a good choice.

- Taking apart and re-sewing a book is often more simple than trying to work within a bound structure. Don't worry about fancy stitches or knots; just make sure your sewing holds the book together and the knots are tightly tied.

- Working in a pre-bound book stretches it out of shape at the fore edge as ephemera is added. If you can plan ahead to accommodate the additional thickness of these collage materials, remove an equal depth of existing pages. If you are working with a sewn book, the center page of each signature may be removed by carefully cutting or tearing the paper on each side of the stitches and slipping it out.

- If you have already done work on the first half of the folio, tear or cut away the page, leaving enough decorative edge for the thread to continue holding the remainder of the sheet.

- When you are collaging, if an edge looks "raw" against the surface on which it is being placed, tone the edge to match with marker, crayon or paint.

- If your glued-together pages are wrinkled after drying, use a heat source to soften the glue while you apply pressure to flatten. A heat press is ideal, but you can also use an iron or hold a hot air gun in one hand while pressing out the wrinkles with a bone folder held in the other hand.

- Coat the raw edges of a recess with gel medium if they seem to be separating.

Working in a Bound Blank Book

Materials

A blank book that will work with the concept and materials you wish to incorporate into it

Collage, painting, drawing and writing materials of your choice

Decorative materials for the cover, if desired

The blank book that became *Bennington* was completed during a workshop with Julie Graham, a mixed-media artist. During the day I worked with plaster, tar and metal, and in the evening I worked in this inexpensive side-sewn book with corrugated cover.

1. Select art materials that work with the book and concept, and complete the book with images and words.

2. Place a small piece of artwork on the cover, similar to what you have done in the book. Or glue a small object or bit of ephemera to the surface with a heavy-bodied craft adhesive. The corrugated cover of Bennington was embellished with a scrap of rusted metal and a bottle top found in the workshop parking lot.

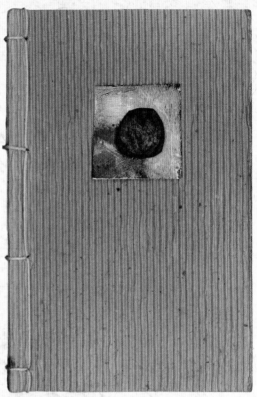

Bennington, 2000, 100 pages, 8¼" × 5¼" (21cm × 13cm)

Pastel and pencil in purchased blank book with brown paper and corrugated cover

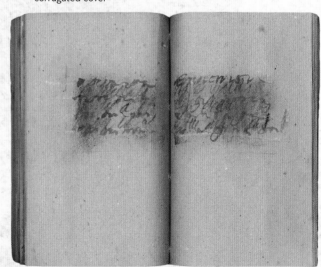

The pages in this book had the quality of brown paper bags. They had a nice texture but were too lightweight for watercolors or acrylics, so I chose to work with pastels and colored pencils. I used alcohol on a paper towel to rub the pastels into the surface of the paper. Because of the materials I had chosen, I could work within the bound book without too much trouble.

Working in an Unbound Blank Book

Fall was made using a blank book with seed pods on the cover and a rough yellow paper, which seemed appropriate for housing autumn leaves I gathered in Maine. If it is easier to work with pages out of the book than bound together, consider taking it apart and re-sewing. When the pages are removed, you can decide to work with fewer pages, or add additional pages of other papers.

Materials

A blank book that will work with the concept and materials you wish to incorporate into it

Collage, painting, drawing and writing materials of your choice

Decorative materials for the cover, if desired

Fall, 2007, 20 pages, 9" × 8" (23cm × 20cm) mixed-media collage in purchased blank book with seed pod cover

1. Decide on the art materials you will use to complete your blank book. For Fall, I decided to incorporate additional papers both as collage materials and as substitute pages with a variety of leaves and gelatin prints of leaves. (See Gelatin Monoprints on pages 30–31.) I also used a collection of rubber-stamped words, including Fragile and Perishable.

2. Select art materials that work with your book's concept, and complete the pages with images and words. In a small metal bowl on a plate warmer, I melted encaustic medium (a mixture of beeswax and resin). I used a cheap bristle brush to cover the surface of a collage with the medium. Since the wax cures almost immediately, I re-melted it with a hot air gun to saturate the collage elements and the paper.

3. When your pages are complete, reassemble the book, punching holes in any new papers by using the old or existing ones as a guide. Straightened paper clips can be put through the holes to aid you in holding everything together. Align the pages with the cover and re-sew. Here, my book was simply re-sewn around twigs that relate to the book content.

ALTERED BOOKS

At the opposite end of the spectrum from the blank book is a book that has already been completed—a turn-of-the-century romance novel, a family recipe book, a book you read as a child, a bank book or ledger, an autograph book, a diary, a passport or a photograph album. Whatever your choice, it should be a book you are willing to transform or adapt for another purpose. Altering an existing book gives you

a ready-made starting point since the book you choose will suggest the content and approach.

Most books I buy come from secondhand bookstores, library book sales or yard sales, and they are very cheap since I'm never sure what I'll do with them. For years, I have had tattered copies of *Uncle Tom's Cabin* and *Alice in Wonderland* waiting for me to decide how to take them to another level of meaning.

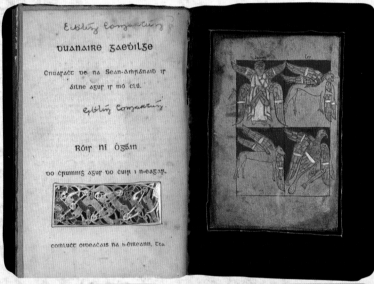

Manuscripts Illuminated, 2002, 52 pages,
6³/₄" × 5" (17cm × 13cm)

Altered book in removable leather paperback cover. Made from a textbook found in Ireland and slipped into a tooled leather cover designed to hold a paperback novel, the pages were collaged as I traveled with images extracted from reproductions of illuminated manuscripts and a box of Celtic rubber stamps.

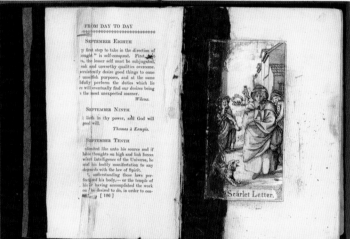

Day to Day, 2000, 17 pages, 9½" × 6¾"
(24cm × 17cm) altered book with mixed media

Day to Day began as a badly deteriorated daybook with "new thoughts." It was altered with mixed media and rebound with the original soft leather cover glued to linen-covered board.

Creative Explorations

- Build a small collection of purchased blank books so that you will always have one to take with you on an impromptu journey or to use to express an idea.

- Consider photograph albums for use as blank books, especially those with high-quality paper inside. They are perfect for collaging since they are designed to accommodate the addition of material at least the thickness of photos.

- For additional interest, incorporate fold-out pages, envelopes to house small items and relatively flat objects of clay, cardboard, metal or natural materials.

- When you take a workshop and make a blank book, choose colors, cover materials or paper that relate to topics you may want to explore. Add it to your collection of possibilities.

- Consider unifying diverse materials with a coat of gel medium or encaustic.

- Look for small items to emb into glued-together pages.

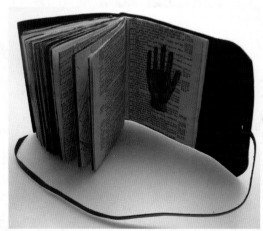

Embedded hand from Promised Land, 2001, 32 pages, 6¾" × 5" (17cm × 13cm)

An Altered Book

Materials

A book that will work with the concept and materials you wish to incorporate into it

Collage, painting, drawing and writing materials of your choice

Decorative materials for the cover, if desired

Glue or adhesive as needed

Scissors

Folder

Title to add to cover, if desired

Optional: scanner, computer, imaging software, printer

For this example, I've chosen to alter *Respectability* by Elbert Hubbard, who began Roycroft Press in 1895 to make beautiful books. Roycroft grew into a utopian craft community with 500 craftsmen making paper, printing, binding books and producing other items of the arts-and-crafts movement. This leather-bound book, letterpress-printed on handmade paper, was found in a used bookstore. The spine had deteriorated and was coming apart.

Because the book dealt largely with the place of women at that time, I decided to alter it in such a way as to only retain the references to women. The first page had an "Apologia," which Maureen Cummins suggested should become the title of this altered book.

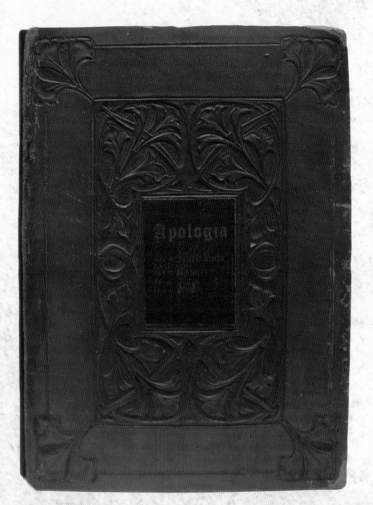

Apologia, 2007, 74 pages, 8" × 5³/₄" (20cm × 15cm) altered book with mixed media based on *Respectability*, leather cover

1. Consider how you can change your book and still relate to its character. Because this book was made around the turn of the century, I decided to incorporate images related to the National Woman Suffrage Association, begun by Susan B. Anthony and Elizabeth Cady Stanton, as well as images from Godey's Lady's Book. I chose to work in rust, brown, beige and black with collage materials, pastels, colored pencils and oil crayons. A tape measure became a recurring icon.

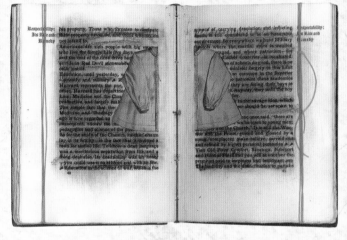

2. Begin to work through the pages, placing your images so that there is both repetition and variation. I decided to leave only the passages related to women readable, and covered over or colored out all the other text. If there were facing pages that had no reference to women, I pasted them together. Where women weren't mentioned for multiple pages, I tore them out to make space for the additional thickness of the added collage materials. The

illuminated capitals were cut from the discarded pages and used as decorative elements. I tried to make the book coherent and flowing from page to page.

If you paste together pages, consider doing something to indicate to the reader that this is deliberate and the pages are not meant to be unstuck. A tab around the edge, a clip or, in this case, a wrapped cord will get the message across.

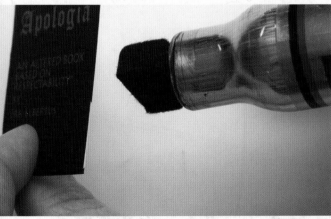

3. If you'd like, change the title on your altered book. I measured the inset on the cover where the leather title had been debossed and, in Photoshop, made a small title plate to cover it. Since I couldn't find an appropriate font, I

scanned the word "Apologia" from the frontpiece and colored it deep rust against a black-brown background. I colored the edge of the print with a black marker and pasted it down with gel medium.

An Altered Book Sculpture

Materials

A book that will work with the concept and materials you wish to incorporate into it

Collage, painting, drawing and writing materials of your choice

Item to embed

Ruler

Gel medium

Heavy-bodied clear adhesive, like E-6000 or Goop, if needed

Snap-blade or craft knife

90° triangle

Folder

Weight

You can turn an altered book into a simple sculptural piece by gluing pages together. In the process, you are creating a thickness that can accommodate an inlaid item in a cutout recess.

The book being altered in this demonstration was "a school and family primer" published in the mid-1800s. It held little interest for me, except for the one double-page spread I decided to use, so it was an ideal candidate with which to make a double-page sculptural form that would remain permanently open.

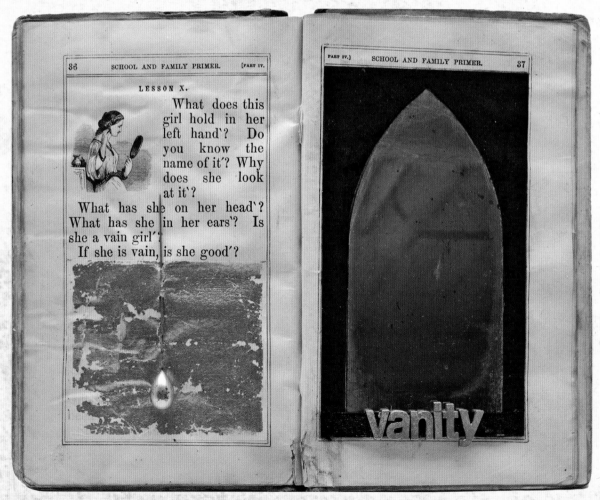

Vanity, 2007, 7½" × 9½" (19cm × 24cm) altered book sculpture with embedded mirror

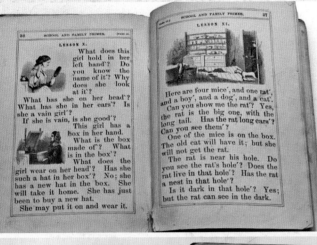

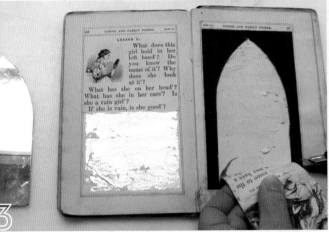

1. Choose a double-page spread for a sculptural form. The page I chose shows a picture of a young woman lifting an earring to her ear as she looks into a mirror while the text asks, "Is she a vain girl? If she is vain, is she good?"

2. Coat the inside front cover with gel medium and press the first page against it, smoothing it down evenly and burnishing from the spine to the edges with your folder. Glue each of the pages in succession until you have a solid block with your left-hand chosen page on top. Moving to the inside back cover, repeat the process until the back half of the book is also a block. Dry the book under weight.

3. Select collage, painting or drawing materials to help you take your chosen pages to another level. With gel medium, I've glued a piece of silver joss paper over the unrelated text on the left side and glued a piece of black paper to cover text and image on the right.

If you have an item to embed, measure the height, width, depth and placement for an embedded item. Use a 90º triangle to draw straight angles for a square or rectangular recess, or draw around a shaped item for an irregular recess. Cut the recess by making many shallow cuts through the pages with a craft knife with a pointed blade if a snap-blade knife is too large.

To embed a thin mirror into this relatively slim book, I cut through to the back cover with a snap-blade knife. An item with more depth would have required a thicker book.

Remove the pages from the center area to create the recess by lifting with the tip of your knife.

4. If you are embedding a relatively flat-bottomed and light item, it can be adhered to the recess with gel medium; otherwise, use a heavy-bodied craft adhesive.

At the last minute, I decided I preferred the gold-toned back of the mirror and embedded it facedown. It wasn't quite symmetrical, so I had to trim out a bit more to make the right side fit and color a bit of exposed paper with black marker.

You can also add other elements to complete the composition. The metal letters that spell "vanity" were slipped over a black ribbon and adhered to the surface of the mirror bottom with double-stick tape. A hatpin with a large pearl was skewered through the pages.

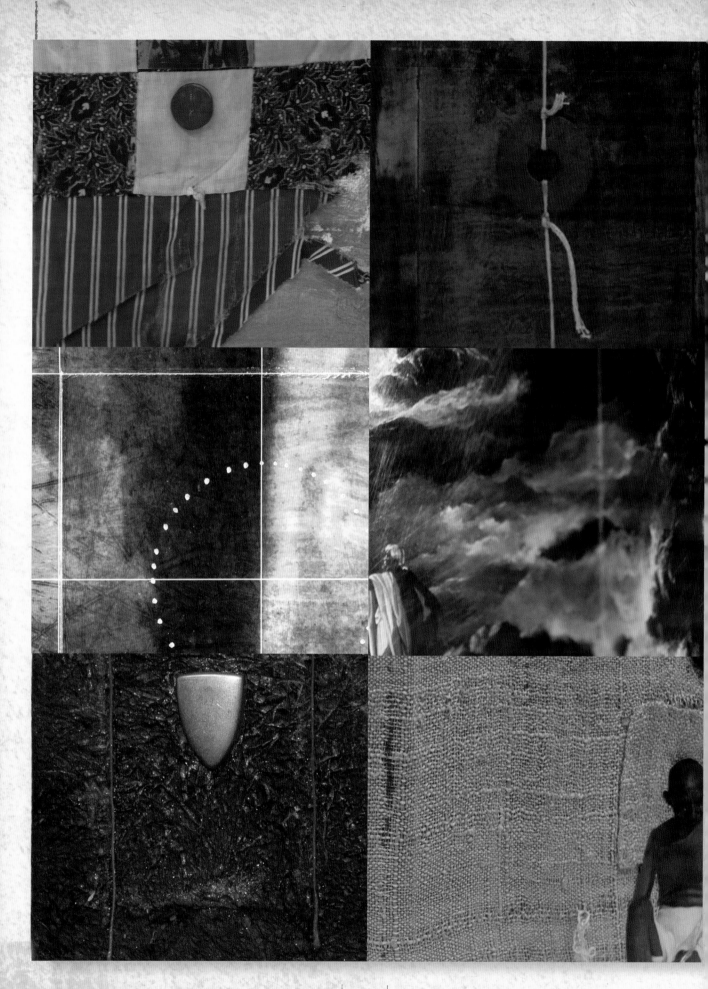

SINGLE-FOLD, BI-FOLD AND BOOKS FOLDED FROM ONE SHEET

Some of the simplest structures for artist books are constructed from a single sheet, or from smaller sheets that have been assembled to function as a single sheet. They can be folded into interesting map-like or origami-like forms. The order and direction in which the folds are made determine the order of the smaller folded pages and serve to compact and "close" the book. Using a substrate that works with your chosen structure, you can quickly and easily assemble your images and words into book forms. In the next chapters, we'll work with single-fold and bi-fold books, books folded from a single sheet, concertina or accordion-fold books and scrolls, and we'll make an interesting assortment of structures.

Patriot Act, 2007, 2 pages, 5½" × 3½" × 1½" (14cm × 9cm × 4cm)

Single-Fold and Bi-Fold Books

Single-fold and bi-fold books are extremely simple structures with great potential. A single fold is a sheet folded once to create two inside and two outside pages—a folio. And a bi-fold sheet is folded twice to create three inside and three outside pages—an altar-like, three-panel form. Because they can stand and be viewed from all sides, we'll also explore the impact of that form of presentation in this chapter. And, since there are wonderful found objects like folders and boxes that lend themselves to this format, we'll also look at some substrates other than paper.

playing around, 2001, 2 pages, 5½" × 4½" (13cm × 11cm) mixed-media folio
A single-fold book with metal feet made from vintage photo album pages, antique playing cards and pieces of an Erector set became playing around. The cover is made from black unryu paper rubbed with silver pigment, trimmed with thin red ribbon and a silver found metal object.

 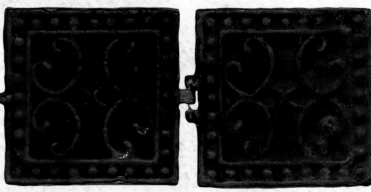

Arabesque, 2008, 2 pages, 4¾" × 4¾"(12cm × 12cm) cast iron and polymer clay with metallic pigment
Arabesque was a found, hinged, cast-iron piece with a repeating geometric form. A thin sheet of polymer clay was pressed against the inside surface, baked and rubbed with metallic pigment to fill in the open spaces and enhance the abstract design.

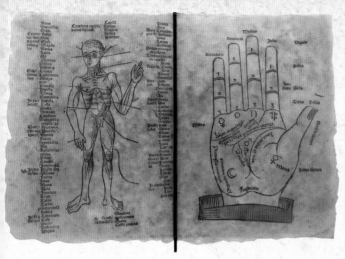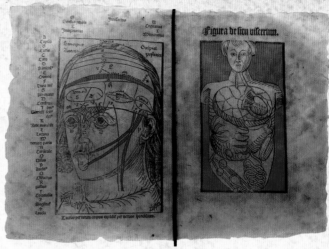

Hundt, 2006, 2 folios, 21" × 30" (53cm × 76cm) inkjet print on handmade lama li paper transparentized with encaustic

Hundt was produced during my artist-in-residence at Harvard Medical School's Countway Library. Printed on large sheets of handmade paper, it was heavily soaked with wax to make it translucent, and each folio hung with decorative pins pushed through a leather spine.

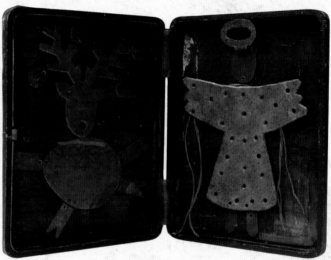

tis the season, 2006, 2 pages, 7³/₄" × 6" (20cm × 15cm) mixed-media in leatherette box

Two rusty metal folk ornaments, a reindeer and an angel, were taken apart so they could be flattened and glued into a found leatherette box. A bit of red raffia and a square of silver oriental joss paper were added. A title embossed with a labelmaker into a red plastic strip was colored with a gold marker and highlighted with silver Rub 'n Buff.

Weaver, 2004, 2 pages, 7" × 5³/₄" (18cm × 15cm) mixed-media with a handwoven cloth cover

Weaver was made from a vintage wood cutout of Mahatma Gandhi and world leaders found in India. It was collaged onto board covered with handwoven fabric.

Arles, 2006, 3 pages, 9½" × 6½" (24cm × 17cm) closed, 9½" × 13" (24cm × 33cm) open, edition of 40

Arles was completed in Provence in 2006. The structure was a purchased lama li folder with a bamboo closure and a duplex paper of rich orange on the outside and black on the inside. The maps of the area came from a Baedeker's Southern France guidebook published in 1914, and the carrot was the symbol of the 2006 Arles International Photo Festival. After it was completed, I decided to edition it as a thank you to many of the participants in the event that prompted the trip. The original was scanned and printed, back and front, on heavy fine-art paper.

Altar, 2001, 3 pages, 7½" × 4½" (19cm × 11cm) mixed-media on wood

Altar began with an inexpensive Italian hinged wooden triptych. Collage elements were added, then the entire piece was darkened and aged by rubbing with burnt umber oil paint and wax.

lamentations, 2002, 3 pages, 6³/₄" × 6" (17cm × 15cm) closed, 6³/₄" × 12" (17cm × 30cm) open, edition of 20

The cover of lamentations is a photograph of a 4' (1m) tall copper diptych, *In the Name of the Mother*. When the original idea was conceived, I made images to transfer to both the outside and the inside of these surfaces, but because the inside needed cross-bracing, the interior images were never used. So I decided to make a book using the three images. The images were glued to bookboard, which functioned as the outside and inside of doors. Hinged with strips of black gaffer's tape, the doors open to reveal a black centerpiece with a lead symbol of Pisces, referencing the twin performance artists in the photographs, Emily and Abigail Taylor.

Interior Landscapes, 2001, 3 of a series of 6, each 5¹/₄" × 4¹/₄" (13cm × 11cm) closed, 5¹/₄" × 8¹/₂" (13cm × 22cm) open

Bi-fold collages on black mat board, designed to stand. They were heavily textured with encaustic and rubbed with metallic pigment.

Helpful Hints

- When you are scoring to fold a bi-fold, take into account the thickness of the fold and make sure the outer pages will meet in the center.

- If you are using thick items in your folio book, allow extra board to make a spine with adequate thickness to accommodate the collaged items.

- If you want your book to stand, consider the size of your pages and the weight of the materials when making single- and bi-fold structures. Large pages of lightweight materials may be too floppy to remain upright.

- If you are going to print images or text on your sheet before folding, make a sample first to ensure that the orientation is correct and your printed pages won't be upside down.

- When printing the front and back of pages, first print a light gray outline on an inexpensive sheet of paper, and then turn it over and print the back side to check for alignment. Some printers align perfectly every time, while others never seem to begin at the same point twice. Try feeding the paper from the paper tray or the front or rear flat feed, if your printer has one, to see which aligns best.

- If alignment is difficult when printing on the front and back, use an image that is different on each side.

SINGLE-FOLD FOLIO

Materials

Paper, heavy sheet or mat board

Collage, painting, drawing and writing materials of your choice

Glue or adhesive as needed

Pencil

Folder

Ruler

Snap-blade or craft knife

One of the simplest structures that can be called book-like is a two-page single-fold, or folio. It can be hung, or made of paper or board heavy enough to stand, and it can also function as an object.

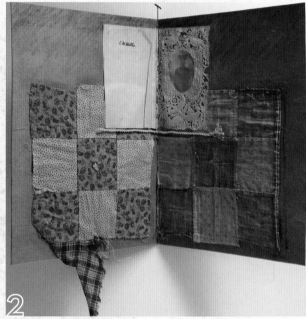

1. Choose images or items that tell a story or make a comment. I decided to use pieces from an unfinished print and a few collages using old photographs and quilt squares. I called the piece *Remnants*.

2. Decide on a size, determine the center of the board, score with a folder and make a fold that will function as the spine or hinge. Since my collage was symmetrical, I folded it in half and, using a craft knife, trimmed it to a size I felt would work as a standing or hanging book. I glued the collage to a heavy backing sheet with gel medium.

3. On the outside, add related images or items for the cover. I decided to layer another piece of the silvered print to the cover to give a sense of dimensionality. I used a silver gel pen to draw into stencil letters, and add a title.

Bi-Fold Book

With an additional fold, a bi-fold book may reveal its contents one section at a time. It may also have more substance as a standing object since its three-part base is more secure. Since I had additional pieces from the construction of the single-fold *Remnants*, I decided to make a companion piece as a bi-fold and call it *Remains*. I often work with series of images using related materials and letting each piece suggest the next.

Materials

Paper, heavy sheet or mat board

Collage, painting, drawing and writing materials of your choice

Glue or adhesive as needed

Pencil

Folder

Ruler

1. Choose images or items that tell a story or make a comment. Decide on a size. Divide the width of your piece by four. Score only the left and right sections with a folder. Make folds on the scored lines that will function as hinges. Close the outside sections toward the middle and press the folds.

2. I decided to use a 12" × 18" (30cm × 46cm) sheet made by gluing the silver paper (for the inside) to brown paper (for the outside) with acrylic gel medium. I measured the 18" (46cm) width into four 4½" (11cm) divisions. I scored the along each of the outside measurements with a folder and folded the 4½" (11cm) pieces toward the center. A collaged quilt square, similar to the one used in *Remnants*, was glued to the inside center, and stencil letters were used on the outside cover.

BOOKS FOLDED FROM ONE SHEET

There are many variations on books folded from a single sheet. In these examples, they are relatively large sheets that, when opened flat, could hang on a wall or, if folded into a compact structure, could be easily transported. One of the simplest examples would be a map. If you make one or more cuts into the sheet, it can take on a different, more book-like configuration. By working with images on the front or the back of your sheet, different fold patterns and different cut placements, you can create a wide variety of structures. Because of the number of folds, grain is irrelevant and, unless you want it to stand, a lightweight, uncoated paper works best. What is covered in this section is just the beginning. If you begin to think of origami, there are endless three-dimensional possibilities. Paper artists are using three-dimensional tessellation structures, box pleating and stretched pleats to create amazing pieces with the potential to relate to book forms.

The illustrations here show diagrams with page numbers printed on the bottom of each sheet, red lines indicating cuts to be made and examples of the folded book form. In the finished pieces, the size of the original sheet is listed in parentheses.

If your sheet has images or text with an orientation, like the landscape in *Cooks Straight* or the writing in *Declaration*, take it into consideration when planning your layout. Images that can work in any direction make your task simpler.

91	SL	⊅L	EL
9	10	11	12
8	∠	9	S
1	2	3	4

Movement, 2007, 16 pages, 3" × 4¼" (7cm × 11cm) closed, 3" × 46¼" (7cm × 117cm) open, single sheet folded music score (12" × 18½" [30cm × 47cm])

cover	back	9	5
1	2	3	4

Cooks Straight, 2007, 6 pages, 5¼" × 4" (13cm × 10cm) single sheet folded painting (10½" × 16" [27cm × 41cm])

Cooks Straight, a six-page pamphlet, was made from a folded and sanded reproduction of a painting by William Hodges that recorded the voyages of Captain Cook in the late 1700s.

9	10	11	12
8	7	6	5
1	2	3	4

Declaration, 2007, 12 pages, 5¼" × 3½" (13cm × 9cm) closed, 5¼" × 27¾" (13cm × 70cm) open, single sheet folded (15¾" × 13¾" [40cm × 35cm])

A facsimile of the Declaration of Independence with a facsimile of Massachusetts currency became *Declaration*, a twelve-page ox plow.

Materials

Paper, any size or shape, with or without images and text

Ruler

Pin

Folder

Snap-blade or craft knife

Cutting mat

Your books can be made with blank paper and then completed with content, or you can use paper with imagery and text either placed in such a way that the orientation of the folded pages is irrelevant, or plan for the content to fit the folded pages. A quickly made sample will make it easier to see some of the possibilities. The images in these two demonstrations can work in any direction.

In the six-page demo, *Starbright*, the cover, back and all the visible pages are on the same surface. The paper was a Christmas party favor—a composite sheet of star drawings by the children of residents at the American Academy in Rome.

In the twelve-page demo, *Landsquares*, the cover and back are on the reverse surface. The same image was printed on both sides of a 13" · 16¼" (33cm · 41cm) sheet, full bleed. To get the straightest, sharpest folds, remember to press each fold with your folder and open the sheet flat before going on to the next step.

SIX-PAGE FOLD

1. Fold the sheet of paper in half lengthwise, press the fold with a folder and open the sheet flat. Fold the sheet of paper in half crosswise, press the fold with a folder and open the sheet flat. Fold each crosswise half of the sheet toward the middle to divide it into fourths, press the folds with a folder and open the sheet flat.

2. Open the page flat and cut along the lengthwise fold between the outer two pages as shown in red on the six-page diagram. The ends of the cut have been marked with pinpricks.

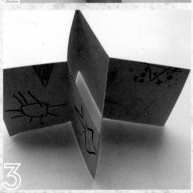

3. Fold the sheet in half lengthwise. With the cut side up, push the two ends toward the middle to make a plus-sign shape. Push the center sections to the right to enclose the right section. Bring the single remaining section around to the right to form the front cover of your book. Flatten all the folds with a folder.

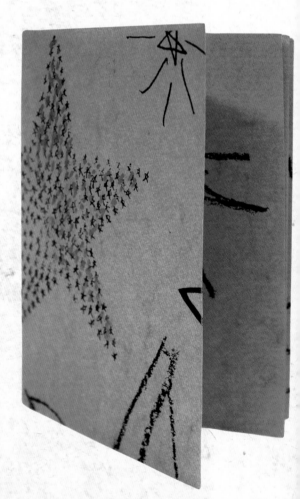

Starbright, 2008, 6 pages, 5½" × 4¼" (14cm × 11cm) pamphlet folded from a single sheet (11" × 17" [28cm × 43cm])

Twelve-Page Fold

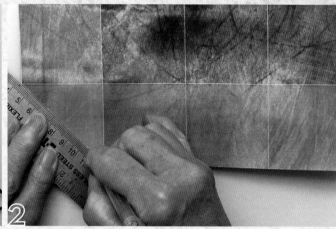

1. Fold the sheet of paper in half crosswise, press the fold with a folder and open the sheet flat. Fold each crosswise half of the sheet toward the middle to divide it into fourths, press the folds with a folder and open the sheet flat. Measure the width of the sheet and divide into thirds. Fold the sheet into three lengthwise strips, press each fold with a folder and open the page flat. Mark the two lengthwise folds from the outer edge to the beginning of the page on the opposite side. Cut along the folds, leaving the outer pages uncut at each end as shown in red on the twelve-page diagram.

2. While you can work out which pages will be up and which will be down in advance and plan your illustrations and text to orient in the proper direction, it's often easier to use imagery that can be viewed in any direction and add final touches after the book is folded.

3. Beginning at one end, fold each page consecutively, turning from one row to the next as if you were an ox plowing the field. Flatten all the folds with a folder.

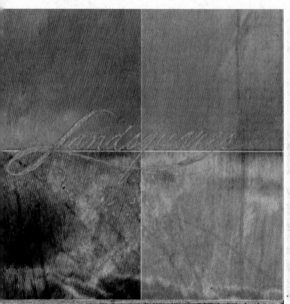

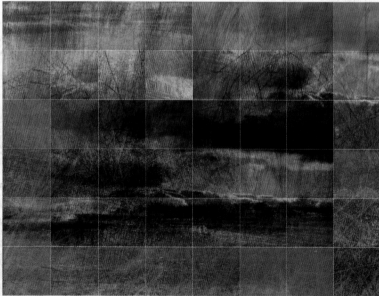

andsquares, 2007, 3¹/₄" × 3¹/₄" (8cm × 8cm) closed, 3¹/₄" × 26" (8cm × 66cm) open, inkjet print on both sides of paper (13" × 16¹/₄" [33cm × 41cm])

ACCORDION BOOKS AND SCROLLS

The accordion-fold book is made from a piece of paper longer than wide and folded into pages to resemble the instrument for which it is named. A favorite of many visual artists, myself included, the accordion can be designed to stand or hang so that the entire book can be seen at once, increasing its visual impact. It's a good structure for telling a story or presenting a related collection of images or objects. A variation of the accordion, the concertina, may have folios attached to the peaks or valleys of the folds. It is also used as the basis for a variety of other structures, including flag books and tunnel books. Pop-ups, cutouts, fold-outs and irregular top edges are some of the many variations of both accordion and concertina books.

Traditionally, scrolls were divided into pages often made from separate sheets glued together. Papyrus, which gives us our word "paper," was used in ancient Egypt and parchment, the treated skin of animals, or vellum, the skin of younger animals, was used in parts of the Mediterranean. In ancient Asia, calligraphy and images were painted on silk.

If the scrolls were horizontal, they were unrolled to expose a single page in sequence, with the remaining pages rolled to the left and right of the visible page. While some scrolls were simply rolled pages, others had rollers on one or both ends. Scrolls were also designed to hang vertically and to function as decorative hangings with images and no text. Eventually, the Romans found scrolls too cumbersome for long works and developed the codex, a bound book with pages.

Once you begin to think about scrolls, you will find concepts that lend themselves to this presentation, and paper, fabric and synthetics that lend themselves to being rolled.

Bingo, 2005, 6 pages, 5½" × 4½" (14cm × 11cm) closed, 5½" × 27½" (14cm × 70cm) open, in box 5¼" × 6" × 1¼" (14cm × 15cm × 3cm)
The game cards from a vintage bingo set were hinged together with tape and altered with silver leaf, metal, red and black paper, paint and bingo chips. This accordion, made on a trip to Las Vegas, is housed in a leatherette-covered traveling box, which also contains the spinner.

Accordion Books

The accordion is a simple structure to make. The height, width and number of pages making up the length of the overall piece will be governed by your content, although you will need an even number of pages to make the covers function properly. Score and fold your pages with the first page coming forward and the next going back, alternating until you have made all of the folds. Press each fold with your folder to make them straight and sharp.

During a particularly productive month as a visiting artist at the American Academy in Rome, I made nine books, four of which were concertina formats: *Tiber, Trastevere, One Square Mile* and *Palladio*.

Arches black cover is a heavy weight paper I often use for accordion books, as seen in *Milagros, Jerusalem* and *Guardians*. Although heavy paper can stand without a cover (as with *One Square Mile*), it is often helpful to have the additional support of mat board, binder's board, wood or other rigid material. You may use a colored or painted board (as with *Trastevere*), or cover it with another material (as with Tiber in leather or *Vengeance is Mine* in lead). You may also house them in boxes (as with *Palladio, Milagros* and *Guardians*).

Tiber, 2005, 6 pages, 5" × 5" (13cm × 13cm) closed, 5" × 25" (13cm × 64cm) open

A piece of hand-marbled paper reminiscent of the river flowing through Rome became Tiber. It has additional marbled paper on the back, and a metallic leather cover with a rub-on type title.

Trastevere, 2005, 16 pages, 6¹⁄₂" × 4³⁄₄" (17cm × 12cm) closed, 6¹⁄₂" × 38" (17cm × 97cm) open, images on back and front

A book on Trastevere, found at the Porta Portese flea market, served as the source for architectural drawings, maps and etchings. The black-and-white images, incorporated into this concertina book made of Arches black cover, were toned and emphasized with copper leaf and copper foil. The cover is black mat board.

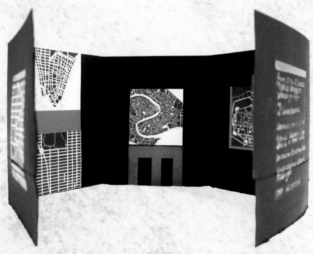

One Square Mile, 2005, 5 pages, 4¹⁄₂" × 4" (11cm × 10cm) closed, 4¹⁄₂" × 20" (11cm × 51cm) open, images on back and front

One Square Mile was based on a presentation at the American Academy by Allan B. Jacobs, "Public Benefit: Places for Life." It compares the number of "intersections" in major cities in one square mile. It is a modified concertina form, arranged to stand in a semi-circular shape designed to enclose the space it describes.

Palladio, 2005, 15 pages, 2³⁄₄" × 2³⁄₄" × 1¹⁄₂" (7cm × 7cm × 4cm) closed, 1³⁄₄" × 26" (4cm × 66cm) open, images on back and front

A small wooden box rubbed with copper pigment became an homage to architect Andrea Palladio. A sheet of paper with Latin text was used as the background for vignettes of his architectural masterpieces. There is a transfer to fresco on the box lid, leather inside the box and a copper medallion on the book cover.

Milagros, 2005, 3" × 2" × 1½" (7cn × 5cm × 4cm) closed, 3" × 24" (7cm × 61cm) open

In Spanish, milagro means "miracle," and the small metal objects called by that name are often nailed to crosses or placed in churches as requests or offerings. A mirrored metal box found in Santa Fe became the container for a collection of old milagros that were attached with glue, wire and string to a structure of heavy black paper.

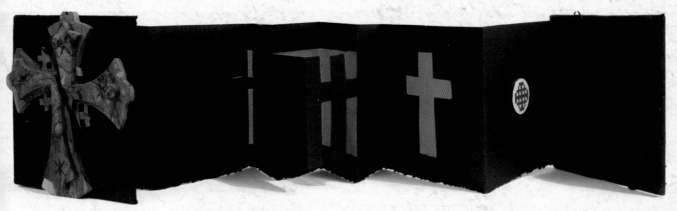

Jerusalem, 2003 4½" × 4½" (11cm × 11cm) closed, 4½" × 27" (11cm × 69cm) open

Jerusalem uses cutouts, pop-ups, translucent red Mylar and objects I gathered in Israel. The components are all related to this divided city claimed as the birthplace of two of the world's major religions. The light through the Mylar gives the effect of stained glass.

Guardians, 2004, 10 pages, 6¼" × 5" (16cm × 13cm) closed, 6¼" × 28" (16cm × 71cm) open

In Bombay, I found a wood and metal box and a series of embossed metal "household guardians," which came together quickly as Guardians.

SIMPLE ACCORDION

Materials

Paper, long enough to accommodate your images and heavy enough to stand, that will be folded into eight pages

Folder

Collage, painting, drawing and writing materials of your choice

Materials for the cover, if desired

Glue or adhesive as needed

Hearts was made as a Valentine's Day gift for my husband. The idea began with a group of slightly irregular hand-cut metal hearts found in a consignment shop.

For the covers, I embedded two hearts and a crossed chain into a thin layer of textured polymer clay wrapped around plywood. It was baked to harden.

1. Choose the images and text you want to use on both sides of the folded paper. Along with a collection of hearts, I used a small tintype, handwritten vintage text and hearts cut from paper. Fold your accordion into an even number of pages. I began by folding my 7½" × 30" (19cm × 76cm) sheet in half lengthwise, then pressed each fold with my folder. I next folded each of the halves into two 7½" (19cm) sections, then folded each of those in half, for a total of eight pages. Add images and words to the individual pages. All elements were glued onto the inside of my book with gel medium and craft adhesive. I left the opposite side of the paper blank.

Hearts, 2007, 8 pages, 7½" × 3¾" (19cm × 10cm) closed, 7½" × 30" (19cm × 76cm) open, mixed-media accordion

I decided to make an accordion book from a tarot card deck I made a decade ago. Since the deck has twenty-two major arcana, or trump cards, I needed more pages than a single sheet of paper would accommodate.

To enhance the presentation, I used the same bag in which the deck of cards was sold. It was large enough to also hold a small booklet describing the history of the tarot and the meaning of the cards.

Materials

Paper, two or more sheets long enough to accommodate your images and heavy enough to stand, that will be folded into an even number of pages

Ruler

Snap-blade or craft knife

Cutting mat

Glue or adhesive as needed

Paper, waxed

Paper, scrap or other clean waste paper

Weight

Clamps or paper clips

Folder

Collage, painting, drawing and writing materials of your choice

Materials for the cover, if desired

Bag, box or other container, if desired

1. Fold your accordion into an even number of pages. Knowing how many pages I needed to accommodate the tarot cards, I folded two lengths of paper and numbered each sheet with the corresponding number of the card. To glue the two lengths together, I overlapped them in the middle, as shown, with paper clips. The overlap left me with an uneven number of pages, so I decided to glue together the front two sheets to make the cover more substantial. The folded cover, on the left-hand side, is also indicated with a paper clip.

2. Add your images and text. Here, the back of each card was covered with gel medium and positioned on its corresponding page. When one side was completed, it was folded together with waxed paper between each page and left under a weight overnight. The back side was completed the following day. The folded front cover was double-thick paper, and the back cover stood well on its own.

Millennium, Tarot, 2008, 28 pages, 6½" × 3¾" (17cm × 10cm) closed, 6½" × 52½" (17cm × 133cm) open, collaged concertina with accompanying booklet in bag 8" × 5½" (20cm × 14cm)

Editioning

Many artist books are one-of-a-kind, but if you want to make duplicates of your book to share with others, you are creating an edition. A limited edition states a fixed number that will not be exceeded, while the unlimited edition has no preset limit. Book artists who spend a year or more conceiving of and producing a book may choose to edition it, especially if they are working with letterpress and printing processes that are relatively easy to replicate. It makes the lengthy production time more cost-effective for sales. My editioned work is sold through Viewpoint Editions.

Since I much prefer to spend my time making a new book over replicating one, I have editioned very few books. However, *Vengeance is Mine* is based on a series of mixed-media pieces, *body + soul*, which began with photographs of twin performance artists Emily and Abigail Taylor. Several groups of work, in different media, were suggested by their various costume changes. As I worked on the art, some of the photographs, printed on a laser printer, lay on my desk. After looking at them for a very long time, I cut away the backgrounds and put them onto a strip of black Arches cover. I painted over them with encaustic, and spattered them with

black ink. Lead, both beautiful and dangerous, was wrapped around wood to become the front and back covers. A found metal object was placed on the front cover, ribbon was used to tie the accordion format together and a single copy of *Vengeance is Mine* was completed.

But because there were a number of people involved in the photo shoot, I decided to replicate the book as a gift for all the participants. I scanned each of the pages and put them together in Photoshop. After listening to an interview of mothers whose sons had been suicide bombers, I decided to add text—conceived in deception, precious cargo, stalked by hate and sacrificed to a vengeful god. Two additional pages to incorporate a title and a colophon were added to the final file, which was printed on an inkjet printer. Onto the lead covers, I nailed inexpensive copper medallions of lilies that I had found at a jewelry supply outlet and patinaed with ammonia. It seemed appropriate that lilies reference life.

Vengeance is Mine, prototype, 2002, 8 pages, 4½" × 4½" (11cm × 11cm) closed, 4½" × 29" (11cm × 74cm) open, lead over wood cover

Vengeance is Mine, 2002, 10 pages, 4½" × 4½" (11cm × 11cm) closed, 4½" × 45" (11cm × 114cm) open, lead over wood cover, edition of 20

Little Red was inspired by a Little Red Riding Hood doll I had as a child. Her skirt flipped over to reveal a wolf, and an embedded music box played "Who's Afraid of the Big Bad Wolf."

On the front side of *Little Red*, I used three Gustave Doré etchings and a phrase from a poem by Ellen Steiber, "Silver and Gold." For the back, I chose to use a longer portion of her poem and a picture of the doll. In part, the poem reads:

Sometimes, I explain,

it's hard to tell the difference

between the ones who love you

and the ones who will eat you alive.

Materials

Paper, long enough to accommodate your images and heavy enough to stand, that will be folded into an even number of pages

Ruler

Snap-blade or craft knife

Cutting mat

Folder

Collage, painting, drawing and writing materials of your choice

Materials for the cover, if desired

Glue or adhesive as needed

Optional: scanner, computer, imaging software, printer

Little Red, 2007, 4 pages, 6½" × 5" (17cm · 13cm) closed, 6½" × 20" (17cm × 51cm) open, edition of 6

1. Decide on the size and number of pages needed to accommodate your images and text. This book was designed at 6½" (17cm) tall and 20" (51cm) long with four 5" (13cm) pages. Fold your accordion into an even number of pages. The large illustration in Little Red was folded in the middle to create a double-page spread.

2. If you are adding a cover, make the board ¼" (6mm) larger than the pages. I printed inkjet canvas 1" (3cm) larger to wrap my board, and scored to fold around the edges. The corners were mitered, and the back of the canvas was coated with acrylic gel medium. The board was placed on the glue-covered canvas, and the excess was folded around to the back and burnished with a folder.

3. The red ink on the printed canvas cracked when folded, so I rubbed brown shoe polish into the exposed white fibers to cover them up and also to create the effect of an old, worn cover. If you are adding covers, glue them to the front and back pages with PVA or gel medium.

SCROLLS

Scrolls are an interesting way to present work that's been created on a variety of surfaces, including parchment, papyrus, paper, fabric or synthetic material. Like altered books, found scroll-like objects can also be used as the basis for scrolls. In the accompanying illustrations, you

see a collection of objects that have the potential for becoming scrolls, including a souvenir from India, a player piano roll, a snakeskin in a clear plastic brush holder and a roll of brown paper with wire in the edges used on large Christmas wreaths.

Helpful Hints

- If you are using images or words from other artists and writers, be sure they are in the public domain, or get permission to incorporate them into your work.

- The bottom of the accordion pages and the bottom of the covers should sit evenly on the table so that the book stands level and doesn't tilt.

- An accordion attached within a box may tend to go downhill when opened if the inside of the box is higher than the table or shelf on which the box sits.

- Although many accordions have nothing on the back side, extending your concept can add significantly to the presentation. After I thought I was finished with *Viewpoint*, I decided to relate to the inkjet print on the front side with a pastel and colored pencil landscape on the back.

- In addition to being dimensionally stable, most synthetic materials don't fray and require no hemming, making them ideal for banners and scrolls.

- Remember, many desktop printers can print up to 44" (112cm) in length—good for accordions or scrolls.

- To tear an oriental paper with visible fibers, use a small, wet brush to draw down the edge of the ruler. This will wet the fiber and weaken it to make tearing easier. Hold the ruler firmly in place as you tear.

- You can use almost any slick surface for sizing fabric. Glass, polypropylene and Formica all work well and, if you're willing to clean them afterward, a shower door or glass slider is usually handy.

- Editioning can be labor intensive and boring. Any templates you can make to speed the process of marking, cutting and folding. will be helpful. Also, instead of completing each book before going on to the next, consider an assembly line where you do all the marking, all the cutting, all the folding. At the opposite extreme, some artists choose to make one book, then, as it is sold, make another to replace it.

Monkey Grip, 2004, 4½" × 16½" (11cm × 42cm) paper collage scroll in box 4½" × 2" (11cm × 5cm) diameter

Year-of-the-monkey laser cutouts were glued onto separate sheets of oriental joss paper then pasted to a continuous backing. After spending time in a cylindrical Monkey Grip tire patch can, the scroll took on an interesting scalloped effect.

olga, 2007, 2¼" × 32" (6cm × 81cm) in clear acrylic container with black ds 2½" × 7½" (6cm × 19cm) scroll of film, printed copper foil and tape

veloped film taken with an inexpensive Holga camera was transformed into a oll with the addition of black tape and printed copper adhesive-backed foil. A ar plastic tube became the transparent housing for this small scroll that is loosely ed so the light will still pass through it when closed.

Fragile, 2007, 5½" × 32" (14cm × 81cm) hanging scroll of fabric and natural material

For a hanging scroll, leaves were sewn into a hollow ribbon with gold thread. As the leaves dried, they became fragile. If this scroll were rolled, the leaves would disintegrate. The ribbon is wrapped and secured with brass brads to a small square dowel with gold-painted ends.

From the Tree, 2007, 1½" × 12" (4cm × 30cm) paper scroll in carved box 3¾" × 3" (10cm × 8cm) diameter

A small scroll was made in Seattle to fit into a wood purchased box made from a hollowed-out piece of tree. The top pivots open on a pin to reveal the inner space.

To Do, 2008, 5½" × 3½" × 1¾" (14cm × 9cm × 4cm) paper scroll (unknown length) on metal hanging stand

A vintage metal stand with a roll of paper for making grocery lists became *To Do*. Rub-on letters, crossed out, were added across the bottom of the paper roll as both the title and a commentary on making lists.

SCROLL ON FABRIC

Materials

Substrate that can be rolled

Sizing material, if needed

Collage, painting, drawing and writing materials of your choice

Glue or adhesive as needed

Brush

Folder

Box or other housing

As you begin to think about making a scroll, consider the various shapes, widths, lengths and range of materials you might use. You can design it to roll or hang vertically or horizontally, to stand, to be unfurled on a surface or to remain in its housing. If you choose to close your scroll, you may attach one or both ends around a core, rod or baton for support, and you may roll it all in one direction or roll each end toward the center.

For another project, I had placed rusting metal on a piece of muslin. I decided to use a leftover piece that resembled faded writing.

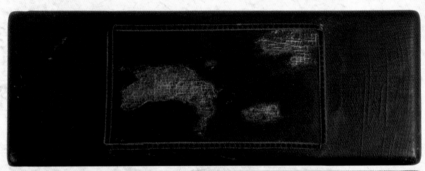

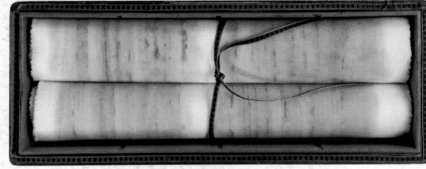

Long ago and far away, 2008, 19½" (50cm) · unknown length, fabric scroll in wooden box 3½" × 20¼" × 2½" (9cm × 51cm × 6cm)

1. Choose a substrate for your scroll that can be rolled. Because the rusted muslin I chose was weak, I laid it against a full-sized mirror, coated it heavily with wheat paste and let it dry overnight. The wheat paste, like starch or sizing, gave the fabric body. In this case, because the fabric edges had been torn, it left the raw edge but stopped any potential fraying.

2. Consider how you will present your scroll. A box, the same length as the width of my scroll, had some shapes on the cover, left by a torn-off paper label, that looked a bit like islands or continents. I decided to enhance them by brushing over the surface with a gold watercolor pigment. I touched a stiff brush into cold wax medium then into the pigment and lightly rubbed it onto the crackled surface. I used a woven fabric trim to wrap around the scroll and tie, to cover the inside edge of the box and to outline the "lands" on the box lid.

Scroll on Nonwoven Fabric

This scroll began with strips of UV-cured ink that were salvaged from the cleaning of a flatbed printer, used primarily for sign-making. Bonny Lhotka thought I might find them interesting, and mailed these fragile paint skins to me rolled around a paper towel core and interleaved with paper towels.

Substrate that can be rolled

Collage, painting, drawing and writing materials of your choice

Nails or staple gun and heavy-duty staples

Glue or adhesive as needed

Brush

Folder

End rods, if desired

Box or other housing

Signs, 2008, 9" × 35" (23cm × 89cm) fabric scroll in box 3³/₄" × 12¹/₄" × 3³/₄" (10cm × 31cm × 10cm)

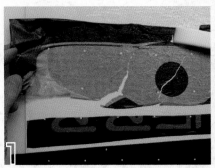  

1. Choose a substrate for your scroll that can be rolled. I chose a piece of textured spun-bonded polyester. I painted pearl metallic on the front and black gesso on the back. I added a bright red ribbon and glued it and the skins to the polyester with gel medium, rubbing lightly with a folder to adhere the fragile skins to the surface.

2. Decide how you will roll your scroll. The box I wanted to use to house this scroll was longer than the scroll was wide, so I decided to adjust the length of two rods to make up the difference. I cut two pieces from a broom handle, sanded the cut ends and painted them with red acrylic paint. I measured and aligned the midpoints and stapled the scroll to the rods so that they would roll toward the center. I coated the rods well with craft adhesive and turned them until the staples were hidden inside the roll.

3. Consider how you will present your scroll. Recognizing that signage was probably the source of my collage materials, I added the title "Signs" to the pasteboard box with a white pencil and a stencil. I underlined the title with a strip of the same red ribbon collaged onto the scroll. When the rolled scroll is placed in the box, with each rod rolled toward the center, only the ends of the rods and the black outside of the scroll are visible. Opened, Signs reveals colorful references to its former life.

PERFECT BINDINGS, DRUMLEAF BINDINGS AND BOARD BOOKS

In this chapter, we'll explore adhesive bindings that have great potential for your books. The most common adhesive bindings are commercial paperbacks: single sheets of inexpensive paper held together with a glue that is not elastic enough for the book to open easily and, with heavy use, allows the pages to fall out. Typically referred to as *perfect binding*, this option is sometimes available at copy centers or can be ordered on the Internet in varying qualities. Handmade adhesive-bound books can alleviate some of these problems by making structural changes in the process and using high-quality paper and glue. If the binding is made using hot glue, it is referred to as a *thermal binding*.

A child's board book is made from images printed on one side of a heavy paper or card stock to produce a double-page spread. Each spread is adhered to the following spread to create a structure designed to take the abuse of handling by small children. A similar but more elegant structure can be made using flexible pages. We'll look at a simplified "board" book and at a variation, the *drumleaf binding*, a term coined by Timothy Ely for the binding he developed. In making books, tape is often a good alternative to liquid adhesives.

Climate Change, 2007, 24 pages, 7" × 5½" (18cm × 14cm) (See pages 122–123.)

PERFECT BINDINGS

If you need a single copy or a small number of commercially produced books or catalogs, there are companies that let you "print on demand." Depending on the company, you either use their software to lay out your book, or you create a PDF file. Most companies offer limited choices in the paper, sheet size, number of pages and binding material, but if you want to produce multiple copies of a book or catalog for an exhibit of your work, it may be a "perfect" solution.

Perfect-style bindings require no sewing and little glue. They are typically comprised of a stack of relatively absorbent single sheets, glued together at the spine with a hot or cold adhesive. We'll look at two possibilities for printing and binding your own materials in a perfect-style, thermal adhesive binding, using hot glue. The first is an inexpensive, commercially available thermal binding system that uses covers with a glue impregnated binding strip. The second binding uses a spine you can make with hot-melt glue and use on your own cover with an electric frying pan as the heat source.

Perfect bindings can be a simple and unobtrusive means of holding together collections of postcards, photographs or sketches.

Scituate, 2008, 14 postcards, 28 pages, 3½" × 5½" (9cm × 14cm)

A collection of vintage postcards held together with black gaffer's tape. Cut to extend just beyond the width of the spine, the glue-impregnated tape was heated in an electric frying pan to melt the glue into the postcard spine.

Helpful Hints

- Hard, coated papers don't absorb glue well. To make them more absorbent, roughen the spine edge of the papers with sandpaper. If you're having your binding done at a copy center, this might be a helpful step.

- If you've made a mistake or later want to change pages, you can put the book back into the warm binder or electric frying pan to soften the glue, take out the old pages and put in others.

- If the bottom of your electric frying pan leaves marks on your book's spine, put a piece of aluminum foil in the bottom of the pan to provide a clean surface.

Egg Money, 2008, 80 pages, 7½" × 4¾" (19cm × 12cm)
Traditionally, one of the few ways a farm wife had to make money was caring for chickens and selling their eggs. A small account book that records fifteen years of income and expenditures in the 1920s and 1930s was placed within a soft cover created with nonwoven fabric, textured with Hydrocal and paint and inkjet printed. With a hot-melt glue strip in the spine, the cover was wrapped around the account book and heated in an electric frying pan to adhere the two together.

Creative *Explorations*

- Use cold glue to make a perfect binding. This technique, using PVA, is sometimes referred to as "double fan" gluing. Align your pages so that the spine edge is square. Clamp the pages between two boards, with the spine edge extending about ¼" (6mm). Push the pages to one side and use a dry bristle brush and thick PVA to paint glue about ⅛" (3mm) into the spine edge. Be sure the glue is thick enough so that it doesn't seep down between the pages. Push the pages to the opposite side and repeat the process. Square up the book block, rub the glue into the spine with your finger and wipe off any excess. Strengthen the spine with muslin or mull if desired, and let the book dry overnight under weight before adding your cover.

- Make books of photographs for special occasions. Depending on the method you choose, it's relatively inexpensive and fast to create perfect-bound books for a special birthday, graduation or retirement celebration. If you're making inkjet prints or color copies, once you have the pages laid out, print enough for all the people you know would want one, or have them printed and bound by an online service.

THERMAL BINDING

Materials

Desktop thermal binding system, like PhotoBook Creator

Cover with spine the thickness of your number of pages and glue embedded (included with the binding system)

Single pages, the dimensions of the cover, with or without images and text

Collage, painting, drawing and writing materials of your choice

Scissors

Glue or adhesive as needed

Desktop thermal binding systems, such as PhotoBook Creator, hold the pages upright in a pre-existing cover while you apply heat that melts a layer of glue embedded in the spine. The glue fuses the edges of the loose sheets to the spine. An introductory kit typically includes the binding machine, two to three hard covers and software to create the appropriate-sized page layouts for approximately $100.

Although you are limited in the trim sizes of these books, you can choose the thickness of the spine to accommodate varying numbers of pages, and you can use the paper of your choice, including pages that have already been completed with image and text.

failed rose, 2007,
10 pages, 8³/₄" × 11¹/₄" (22cm × 29cm)

1. Complete your pages. With pen and gold acrylic ink, I copied an Emily Dickinson poem around the edges of inkjet-printed images that had been enhanced with colored pencil.

2. Embellish the cover, if desired. Here, I used Photoshop to add the title of the book to one of the images, printed it onto the same paper as the pages, cut the excess paper away and glued it to the black linen cover with gel medium. I enhanced the title by adding gold leaf.

3. I glued a ribbon around the book, slipping the glued edges under the endpapers.

4. To bind the pages into the cover, begin by preheating the binder. Collate and align the pages and place them tightly against the glue-impregnated cover spine. Place the book, spine down, into the binder per manufacturer's instructions for the heat to melt the glue embedded in the spine. Remove the book, turn off the binder and let cool.

DIY Thermal Binding

If you don't want to invest in a binding machine, you can make your own glue strips with hot melt glue, put them in your own covers and use an electric griddle or frying pan as your heat source. Glue-impregnated spine sheets can be stored indefinitely, and you can cut a spine length from one as needed.

Crossed uses single sheets with acrylic paste paintings and collagraph prints. A cover of the same paper wraps around the spine in a single sheet.

Materials

Piece of gauze, mull or nylon net

Silicon release sheet or Teflon cookie sheet

Hot-melt glue gun and glue

Paper cover to wrap

Glue strip

Ruler

Pencil

Folder

Scissors

Single pages, the dimensions of the cover, with or without images and text

Collage, painting, drawing and writing materials of your choice

Electric griddle or frying pan

Crossed, 2008, 38 pages, 5½" × 5½" (13cm × 15cm)

1. To create a glue-impregnated spine sheet, begin by placing a piece of gauze, mull or nylon net on a silicon sheet or Teflon cookie sheet. Draw parallel strips of hot glue across the material, about ½" (13mm) apart, using a glue gun.

2. Measure the height of the cover material to be ¼" (6mm) taller than the book—⅛" (3mm) at the head and the tail. Measure the width of the cover paper to wrap around the block of pages, plus extend a bit. Cut or tear the cover to size, and mark the center of the cover width.

Center the page block on the mark and mark the cover at each side of the block. Score lines down the cover at these points and fold sharply.

Cut a piece from the glue sheet the length and width of your spine, with the parallel strips of glue running horizontally across the spine. Place the glue strip between the two folded lines. Collate and align the pages and place them tightly against the glue strip in the cover spine and clamp it all together.

3. Preheat an electric frying pan to 350 degrees. Place the spine flat against the bottom of the frying pan for about ninety seconds for the heat to melt the glue embedded in the spine. Remove the book (turn off the frying pan) and let the book cool.

Drumleaf Bindings and Board Books

"Drumming" refers to the fabrication of vellum books where adhesives are used sparingly to avoid the expansion and contraction of the skins. Instead of gluing the entire surface, the skin is attached to the board along an edge. Drumleaf binding uses this same principle with one-sided double-page spreads (folios). With the folded edges at the spine, the folios are placed next to each other in succession, and the spine is glued together from the outside. Then the back of each folio is adhered to the following folio with a line of adhesive against the spine and another on the fore edge. In this exceptionally strong binding,

the images flow uninterrupted and the book opens perfectly flat.

The "board" book is made even more simply by using tape to adhere the spine and fore edge of each folio to the next folio in succession.

We'll look at variations of the "board" book and the drumleaf as options for making adhesive-bound books by hand. They are particularly appropriate bindings for displaying a group of paintings or photographs that extend across a two-page spread, as nothing gets lost in the gutter and no threads interrupt the image.

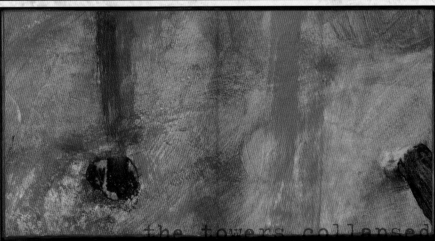

9/11 + 5, 2006, 26 pages, 5³/₄" × 5¹/₂" × 2" (15cm × 14cm × 5cm)

On the fifth anniversary of the attack on the World Trade Center, I made *9/11 + 5*. Acrylic paste paintings and collagraph prints were bound into a drumleaf structure with unglazed clay covers painted with red acrylic and a red kangaroo leather spine. Deciding that the book needed words, I scanned the pages and placed text over them in Photoshop. I then printed the text and transferred it onto the book pages with gel medium.

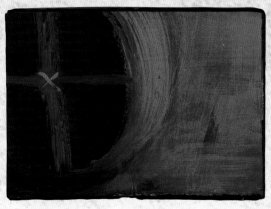

State/Religion, 2006, 18 pages, 7" × 5" (18cm × 13cm)

The text in *State/Religion* refers to the separation of church and state in this country and abroad. It began with acrylic paste paintings and collograph prints on two 22" x 30" (56cm x 76cm) sheets of Arches black cover. The paintings were cut to the size of a cover of polymer clay over wood with a wood and metal collage. The pages were scanned, and images and text were positioned over selected pages using Photoshop. The computer images and text were printed on top of the painted pages prior to binding. The pages were compiled and bound using a drumleaf binding with a gold handmade paper spine.

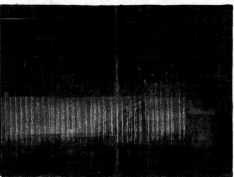

Moral Values, 2006, 18 pages, 6³/₄" × 4¹/₂" × ¹/₂" (17cm × 11cm × 13mm)

Moral Values was made when I was trying to understand why some people find values different from the ones they hold to be unacceptable and try to change them, sometimes by force. This drumleaf has collograph-printed pages and silver-painted unglazed clay covers with a silver leather spine.

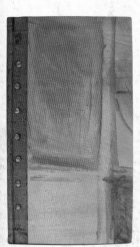

Circle Square Cross, 2006, 20 pages, 9¹/₂" × 5¹/₂" (24cm × 14cm)

Circle Square Cross, another drumleaf binding, is an exploration of the abstract qualities of universal signs and symbols. It has acrylic paste paintings, a cover of paper over board and a bookcloth spine with studs.

Drumleaf Binding

Materials

Double-page spreads (folios), with or without images, cut to size

Folder

Clamps, spring or similar

Strips of rigid material, metal rulers or wood paint stirrers

Glue or double-stick tape

Glue brush

Optional: thin paper with good wet strength

Paper, waxed

Paper, scrap or other clean waste paper

Paper towel

Weight

Chopping mat or other nonabsorbent hard surface

Snap-blade or craft knife

Cutting mat

90° triangle

Sanding block, fine

Painting or drawing material for coloring edges, if desired

This variation of drumleaf binding uses the images that were painted and printed on pages 28 and 29 to produce a book made entirely of double-page spreads. I sequenced my spreads and numbered them on the back in the bottom right-hand corner for assembling. A strip along the top and bottom edges of the spreads was painted on the back so that no white paper would be seen when the book is open.

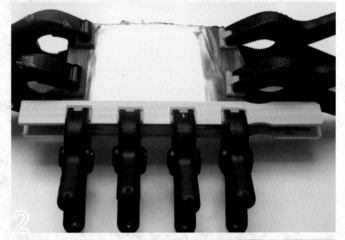

1. Fold the folios and press each spine with a folder. Stack the folios and smack the spine edge sharply against the table so that it is perfectly square. Put clamps on the top and bottom edges and coat the spine with glue. Use a brush to get slightly between the folded spine edges, and then rub the glue into the spine with your finger to ensure that you have a smooth, even coating.

2. Put a strip of rigid material, such as a metal ruler or wood paint stirrer, on each side of the spine to distribute the pressure and keep the clamps from indenting the pages. Hold the spine together with several evenly spaced small clamps until dry.

3. Give the spine additional strength by using glue to adhere a layer of thin paper that has good wet strength, like Kitakata or Tyvek.

4. Place a piece of scrap paper under the second double-page spread and open the page between the first and second image. Paint a 1" (3cm) strip of glue along the length of the spine and a second 1" (3cm) strip along the fore edge. Press the edges together and burnish both spine and fore edges with a folder. Wipe with paper towel if necessary. Throw away the waste paper and get a clean sheet for the next page. Repeat until all pages are glued at the spine and fore edges. Put a sheet of waxed paper between each double-page spread and press under a chopping mat and heavy, even weight over-night or until dry.

5. Place a 90° triangle parallel with the spine and against the edge to be trimmed. Clamp the book and triangle to the edge of a table with a cutting mat

underneath. Cut through the pages with multiple light strokes of a snap-blade knife, cutting away a page or two at a time and extending the blade as necessary to reach to the bottom of the stack. You can choose to trim one, two or all of your edges. In this case, I trimmed only the top edge.

6. Rub over the edge lightly with a fine sandpaper block to remove any irregularities or rough spots. Tone the edges with art materials if needed. You can use pastels, graphite, acrylic paint, gold leaf or other appropriate material.

7. Soften or blend dry materials. To tone the white edges, I rubbed oil crayons into the paper surface with a blending stump. The book block is now ready for a cover, which we will apply on pages 122–123.

Tape-Binding Board Book

Materials

Double-page spreads (folios), with or without images, cut to size

Folder

Tape, Scotch 969 or similar double-faced tape

Scissors

Paper cover to wrap

Ruler or calipers

Pencil

Because you are starting with folios that only have imagery printed on one side, you'll be taping the blank back sides of the folio pages together. Using tape is fast and requires little material, so this is a great method to use while traveling or when in a hurry.

The coastal area south of Boston where I live is known as the "South Shore." This small book focuses on the natural beauty of this area.

South Shore, 2008, 12 pages, 7¹⁄₂" × 8" (19cm × 20cm)

1. Fold the folios and press the spines with a folder. Place a strip of tape along the spine edge and another along the fore edge of the blank back side of your first folio.

2. Remove the protective carrier paper from the tape to expose the adhesive on the spine edge. Align the spine edge of the first folio with the spine edge of the second folio and press the two together. Remove the protective carrier paper on the fore edge and press it to the fore edge of the adjacent folio. Continue adding tape until all the pages are joined at the spine edge and the fore edge.

3. Finish the book with a paper cover. Measure the height of the cover paper to be ¼" (6mm) taller than the book—an extension of ¹⁄₈" (3mm) at the head and tail. Measure the width of the cover paper to be the width of the front plus the back of the book, plus the width of the spine, plus ¼" (6mm)—an extension of ¹⁄₈" (3mm) at the spine edge and the fore edge.

Cut or tear the cover to size. Mark the center of the cover width. Center the spine on the mark and score along each side of the spine. Hold a ruler against one of the scored lines and fold the cover sharply. Do the same against the other scored line to create an indentation.

Open the cover and place the book block against the back inside cover aligned with the indentation. Place tape adjacent to the spine edge of the front page of the block. Place tape adjacent to the fore edge of the front page of the block.

Remove both pieces of carrier paper and close the cover against the tape. Repeat the process to join the book block to the back cover.

 Helpful Hints

- Various art materials can be used to color raw edges. Pastels can be blended with a paper towel dampened with alcohol. If you use acrylic paint, work with a very dry brush to control the amount of moisture being introduced so that it doesn't migrate onto your images or cause the paper to wrinkle.

- If you don't have a 90° triangle, use a carpenter's square.

- Make a sanding block by wrapping a piece of fine sandpaper around a small rectangle of wood.

- If you know you are going to trim edges after gluing, consider what you may be cutting away and plan your margins, text and image placement to accommodate the loss.

- A 3M ATG gun for applying tape will make the process faster and neater.

- It is sometimes difficult to align pages when gluing the spine first. You can add glue and stiffening to the spine after your pages are glued together, or, if you feel it is unnecessary, you can omit that step altogether, as with the "board" book.

- Another way to measure the spine for making lines for scoring is by using calipers or a piece of paper.

- Instead of a folder, use a microspatula or table knife to make a sharper scored line for folding.

Creative Explorations

- Search through your rejected paintings and prints, find one you can see having a second life, cut it into double-page spreads and use them as backgrounds for the pages in your adhesive bindings. Use additional art materials—collage, painting, drawing, printmaking, digital transfers or inkjet prints—to add images and words that will complete your concept.

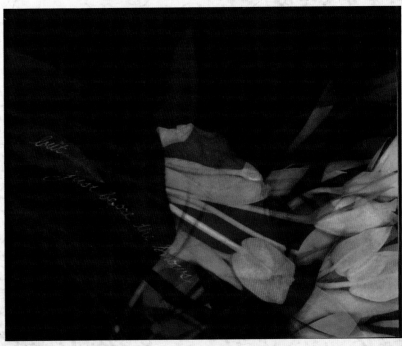

Page from failed rose. (See Demonstration on page 82.)

SIDE-SEWN, SINGLE-SIGNATURE AND MULTIPLE-SIGNATURE BOOKS

Books may be sewn with almost any material that can be threaded through a hole and tied. A heavyweight linen thread that won't break easily is the most common choice, but cord, twine, yarn, strips of leather and ribbon are among the many other possibilities. The color of the sewing materials, what is sewn and how it is sewn can also cover a wide range of options and may become an integral part of the structure. Because this chapter relates to sewing, some general information on sewing tips and knots are presented here.

Side-sewn binding is sometimes referred to as *album* or *stab binding*. It has a somewhat informal feel that I find reminiscent of old photo albums and autograph books. As well as being sewn along the side, this binding can be sewn across the top and can also include other types of fasteners. The side-sewn book has great potential. Don't underestimate it because it's so easy. You can expend your energy on the creative aspects instead of the structure.

What we will refer to as a *signature*, whether a book has one or several, is usually bound by sewing through holes pierced in the spine fold. Instructions for making a piercing cradle are included, and there are instructions for making templates for piercing holes in signatures and spines.

Pages from Solar Cross, 2007, 28 pages 13³/₄" × 13¹/₄" (35cm × 34cm)
Incorporating iconic images of the crossed circle, *Solar Cross* was sewn with a five-hole pamphlet stitch using black linen thread. It was created on 90 lb. (190gsm) printmaking paper, torn across the grain into three folios per sheet with added paste paintings on Mylar. The cover, an inkjet print onto a collage of nonporous materials on aluminum with a patinaed silver tape spine, is shown on page 119.

Sewn Books

Sewn bindings begin with holes that have been pre-pierced with an awl, preferably an awl that has a shaft consistent in diameter so that the holes are all the same size. Pre-pierced holes are a necessity, as they ensure that the pages will be well aligned and help to avoid splitting or tearing during the sewing process.

Needles

Because holes are pre-pierced, most binders use blunt needles. You can buy blunt needles, or blunt the points on sharp needles by rubbing them across fine sandpaper. If you prefer a sharp needle, use a sharp needle.

When choosing a needle, select an eye as small as will allow your thread to pass through. A bookbinder's #18 is a good general-purpose needle that can be purchased blunt or sharp.

The pierced holes—sometimes called sewing stations—should be equal to, or slightly smaller than, the diameter of the needle, so that the thread is held as snugly as possible.

To determine the length of thread you will need, allow one length of thread, equal to the spine length, for each signature and a couple of extra lengths for sewing. It's better to have your thread too long than to come up short and need to add additional thread.

Thread

Thread is made up of multiple strands twisted together. If you can break the thread by holding a piece at each end and pulling sharply, it's not strong enough for sewing a book. Put the end that comes off the spool first through the eye of your needle, then pull and cut the amount of thread you want to use and tie a knot. This will keep the strands going in the same direction that they are twisted on the spool and help you avoid tangles.

To reduce tangling and help stitches and knots hold, drag your thread quickly, several times, across a block of beeswax.

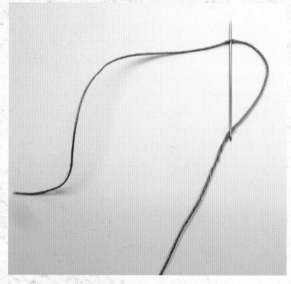

Needle splitting thread fibers

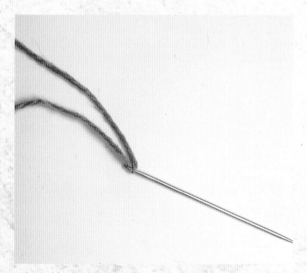

Thread locked without knot

To keep your thread from slipping out of your needle, pass the threaded needle through the short end of the thread, splitting the fibers. Pull it tight. It will hold the thread in place without a knot. (This should be the only time you split your thread. When sewing through a hole a second time, be careful not to split, and weaken, your first thread.)

Knots

You can use any knot that holds when making books, but there are three that work especially well and are worth knowing: the weaver's knot, the overhand knot and the square knot. They're relatively simple, but if you've ever tried to explain in words how to tie a pair of shoes, you know that it's much easier to do than to describe. As you read the following descriptions, practice making the knot with two different colors of fat cord or yarn so that you can see what's happening. To give extra holding power to a knot, put a small amount of PVA or gel medium on a toothpick and rub it into the knot.

Weaver's Knot

A weaver's knot is used to add to a piece of thread that continues in the same direction as the original, so that you can continue sewing. Be sure that it will be in an inconspicuous place, usually in the inside of a signature. Begin by making a loop with the thread you want to add (in the illustration, the black thread). Make a second loop, and pull it through the first loop. Put the end of your old (white) thread through the second loop. Pull both ends of the new (black) thread until they are snug around the old (white) thread, then tighten the knot by pulling the thread being added in the direction away from the too-short thread. Pull tightly until the threads snap in place. If the threads don't snap, the knot won't hold. If you have problems with the weaver's knot, use the square knot instead.

Overhand Knot

The overhand knot is the first half of a square knot. It is used to tie off a single thread when finishing sewing. With two colors of thread, you can easily see what goes over and what goes under. Make a loop with the thread, then bring the loose end through the loop and pull to tighten. If you think you will need more holding power, make a second knot as close as possible to the first. When the overhand knot is tied around a stitch, and both ends are pulled in the same direction, it may be referred to as a *half-hitch*.

Square Knot

To tie two threads together, use a square knot. You may have heard it described as "right over left, under; left over right, under and through." Take the right-hand thread (in the illustration, the black thread) and pass it over the left-hand thread and to the back, or "under." You will have created the top half of the illustration. Then continue with the same (black) thread—now on the left—going over the right (white) thread and under, through the loop now being created to form the knot. The end of each thread will go opposite to the other.

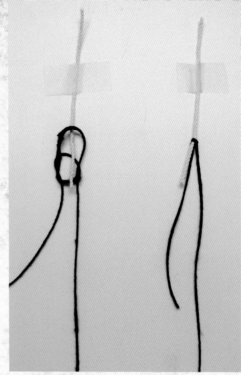

Weaver's knot

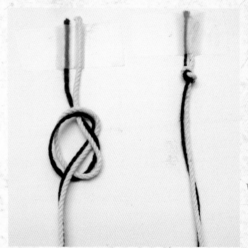

Overhand knot

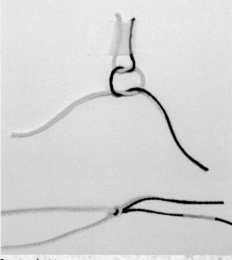

Square knot

Side-Sewn Books

Purchased side-sewn books come in many variations. Photo albums, often with beautiful paper, may be tied with cord or ribbon or have screw posts, sometimes covered by a folding flap. Other side-sewn books may have spiral bindings, or be sewn with decorative stitching patterns. While most have the signatures exposed, side-sewn books may also have covers that wrap the spine, and some have stitching that extends over the edges of the head and tail.

Even more variations are possible when you create your own books. They may be made up of single sheets, sheets folded at the spine or the fore edge, or concertina folds held together so they no longer open into their full length. Asian side-sewn books typically use very lightweight paper folded at the fore edge with the cut edges at the spine. The folded pages and two soft covers are stitched together, often with complex sewing patterns, through holes punched about $1/4$" (6mm) from the spine.

In addition to being held together with braid, leather thong, ribbon, yarn, raffia or other interesting sewing material in a range

of textures and colors, split-pins, brass fasteners that have two legs, can be inserted into punched holes and opened to hold the sheets together. Another holding device is the screw post, a threaded length of metal—typically $1/4$" (6mm) in diameter—with decorative nuts at each end. They are available in different lengths and sometimes with extensions to accommodate even thicker blocks.

An especially useful tool for making large holes in mat board, leather or other surfaces is a screw punch. It has a shaft that rotates as you press down, cutting a clean hole anywhere on your sheet. Most punches come with multiple bits for making holes in several sizes. They make a nice addition to your toolbox.

Generally speaking, side-sewn books don't tend to lie flat and have to be held open while in use. A line scored along the spine creates a fold that may help to lessen the strain on the pages at the holes and help the pages lie flatter. A two-piece cover, hinged on the front or on both the front and back, will provide even greater flexibility.

timeXposure, 1999, 21 pages, 8" × 9" (20cm × 23cm)

A small catalog of inkjet prints of work from the series of the same name, *timeXposure* has single sheets, side-sewn through three holes, in a two-piece cover hinged at the front and back. Watch parts were glued into a rusted metal circle attached to the bookcloth-covered board and also hung from black cord stitching, which goes around a piece of heavy rope. That same rope is used to make a loop that goes over the center circle to hold the book closed.

Biology, 2003, 28 pages, 8³/₄" × 6" (22cm × 15cm)

Biology utilizes altered pages from a sixth-grade biology textbook. Although the stitching over the spine edges is visible, the stitching between the three holes is covered by a leather strip. The bookcloth over binder's board cover has a two-piece hinged front. Polymer clay, a metal heart, leather, ribbons and milagros embellish the cover.

A Year Reviewed, 1999, 88 pages, 7" × 7¹/₂" (18cm × 19cm)

Eight hours on the train, going from Boston to New York and returning, was an opportunity for me to consider what had happened during the previous twelve months. More of a personal journal than an artist book, it incorporated small images of work I had completed and musings on what I hoped to accomplish in the coming year. Some pages were removed, others were added and the two-piece, hinged cover of this purchased book was embellished with found metal.

Side-Sewn Album, Rebound

Materials

Single pages, with or without images and text

Paper for cover

Ruler or calipers

Template for punching holes

Clamps or paper clips

Cutting mat

Screw punch or paper drill

Needle with an eye large enough to accommodate your sewing material, or a dental floss threader

Material for tying book together

Scissors

From 1914 to 1918, World War I, "The Great War," was fought between the Allied Powers of France, the United Kingdom, Russia, Italy and the United States and the Central Powers of Germany, Austria-Hungary, the Ottoman Empire and Bulgaria. The Western Front utilized a system of trenches and fortifications that stretched more than 475 miles. For the first time, planes were used in warfare.

In a secondhand bookstore, I bought a photograph album containing snapshots a soldier took during this conflict. Because the photographs were so badly faded, I scanned all the pages at high resolution, selected some of the images, cropped details to the size of the album and added text from the poem "Back" by Wilfred Gibson. The images and text were printed on sheer vellum paper on a color laser printer and interleaved between the album pages. I chose vellum both because of its ghost-like, see-through quality and because the cover I was reusing would take very little additional thickness.

The one-piece cover wraps around the front and back and is scored for the thickness of the spine and the bends in the pages. I transferred one of the images to the cover with alcohol gel. The following illustrations show pages before and after rebinding.

Back from the War, 2008, 23 pages, 6½" × 9½" (16cm × 24cm)

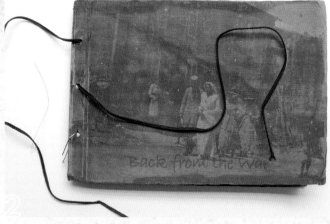

1. Cut a sheet of paper the length of the spine, or use an extra book page for the template. Fold the paper in half crosswise to mark the position where the middle hole for sewing will be punched. Mark approximately 1" (3cm) from the top and 1" (3cm), or slightly more, from the bottom for three holes. Align the pages, place the template at least ¼" (6mm) from the spine edge, clamp or clip them together and place on a cutting mat.

Hold a screw punch or paper drill at right angles to the surface and punch holes, going straight through the template and pages. Since I rebound an existing album, my cover was pre-punched with three holes, and I used one of the album pages as a template to punch through the added sheer vellum interleaving pages. The vellum paper is a much lighter weight than the album pages and has a tendency to slip, so clipping them together is a necessity.

2. Cut two pieces of paper the same size as the book or slightly larger, one for the front and the other for the back cover. Or cut a one-piece cover long enough to wrap around the spine. Use a punched page as a template to mark the holes' placement on the cover, and punch or drill the holes.

Place the pages inside the cover and align the holes. Choose a material with which to sew and choose a stitching pattern. Sew the book together and tie the ends of the sewing material. Although it was originally tied with pink ribbon, I chose a black braid, almost the same diameter as the holes, that seemed more in keeping with the subject matter and the color of the cover and images. The braid was too thick for my needles and almost impossible to get through the holes without a needle because it is heavy and floppy. To pull the braid through the holes, I used a dental floss threader as a needle substitute. This neat tool was discovered by Cherryl Moote, and its use is described in *Books With Girth*.

Although I might have chosen to do a stitching pattern around the spine and the head and tail edges, in keeping with the character of this album, I sewed it with a simple three-hole pamphlet stitch (which is described in detail on pages 105–106). The cord ends are tied together on the cover with a square knot.

Materials

Single pages, with or without images and text

Boards for cover

Ruler or calipers

Pencil

Template for punching holes

Screw punch, paper drill or other drill for board

Snap-blade or craft knife

Cutting mat

Hinge material, paper or fabric for covering

Folder

Glue or adhesive as needed

Brush

Glue

Clamps or paper clips

Needle with an eye large enough to accommodate your sewing material

Thread, cord or other material for tying book together

Scissors

I wanted a book to carry on a drawing expedition, so I gathered a variety of single sheets of handmade papers, and *Sketchbook* was the result. While it doesn't lie perfectly flat, the hinges in the front and back covers give it flexibility and make it reasonably good to work in. And, because the stitching is relatively easy to take out and re-stitch, I can add or remove pages as needed.

Sketchbook, 2008, 28 pages, 8" × 9" (20cm × 23cm)

1. Cut a sheet of paper the length of the spine, or use an extra book page for the template. Fold the paper in half crosswise to mark the position where the middle hole for sewing will be punched. Mark approximately 1" (3cm) from the top and 1" (3cm), or slightly more, from the bottom for three holes. Add two additional holes, for a total of five, by folding from each of the outer marks to the middle mark and adding new marks at the folds.

    Align the pages, place the template at least ¼" (6mm) from the spine edge, clamp or clip them together and place on a cutting mat. Hold a screw punch or paper drill at right angles to the surface and punch holes, going straight through the template and pages.

    Using a screw punch, I punched five holes with the largest size punch I have to accommodate a heavy waxed cord.

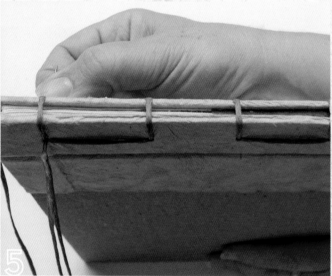

2. Cut two pieces of board ½" (13mm) taller and ¼" (6mm) wider than the size of your pages. Cut 1" (3cm) off the width of the front cover board to make a hinge. Cut a piece of strong paper or fabric for the hinge material, and place the hinge material facedown.

Brush glue over the entire back of the hinge material. Place the 1" (3cm) wide hinge board with the outside edge in the center of the material. Create the hinge gap by placing the front cover board facedown on the glued surface with the distance of the board thickness between them.

3. Turn in the top and bottom margins of the hinge material and press with a folder. Make a good crease into the hinge material at the hinge gap.

4. Add glue to the remainder of the material and wrap it to the inside front cover. Press and crease the material well into the hinge gap with a folder. If the back cover is also hinged, repeat the process. Use a page as a template to mark the holes in the covers and punch or drill holes. Align the pages and cover and hold them together with clamps or clips.

Begin sewing in the middle hole. Leave a 3" (8cm) tail and pass the thread through to the second hole from the head. Go around the spine, coming back through the second hole, being careful not to split the thread. Move to the middle hole and pass the thread through to the other side. Go around the spine, coming back through the middle hole.

5. Continue sewing in, out and around until you reach the tail. Sew around the tail of the book and back through the outermost hole. Stitch in and out through the holes, back to the head. Sew around the head of the book, around the spine and back through the middle of your signatures to the place you began sewing. Tie your two threads together with a square knot and trim the ends of the threads.

Scored Cover

Materials

Single pages, with or without images and text

Back and front covers of paper the size of your sheets, or ¼" (6mm) taller and wider

Ruler or calipers

Pencil

Template for punching holes

Clamps or paper clips

Cutting mat

Awl, screw punch, paper drill or other drill

Needle with an eye large enough to accommodate your sewing material

Thread, cord or other material for tying book together

Scissors

Folder, microspatula or table knife

Will combines a handwritten last will and testament with interleaved prints of nine photographs taken by Viola Käumlen of the Capuchin Catacombs in Palermo, Sicily. The author of this handwritten will leaves to his wife a "right of dower" and "during her life" the use of a sum of money "held in trust."

Will, 2008, 18 pages, 12" × 7" (31cm × 20cm)

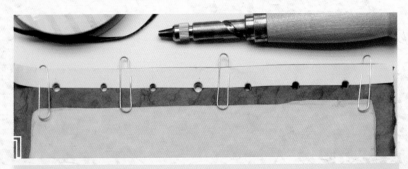

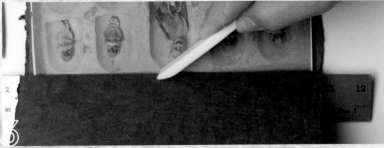

1. For a template, either cut a sheet of paper the length of the spine or use an extra book page. Fold the paper in half crosswise to mark the position where the middle hole for sewing will be punched. Mark additional holes from the left and right edges about 1" (3cm) apart, as desired.

   Align the pages, place the template at least ¼" (6mm) from the spine edge, clamp or clip them together and place on a cutting mat. Hold an awl or paper drill at right angles to the surface and punch holes, going straight through the template and all of the pages.

2. Beginning in the middle front, and leaving a 3" (8cm) tail, sew in and out of the holes from the center to the outer edge. Go around the edge and sew in and out coming back to the middle. Continue sewing in, out and around the opposite edge, and returning to the middle. Slip your needle under the first stitch and tie the ends together with a square knot.

3. Place a ruler approximately the same distance below the holes as the distance above and score against the ruler. Open the cover and press with a folder against the ruler edge. Fold each page against the open cover and press with a folder to crease lightly.

Single-Signature Books

The form of sewn book most common to us is the codex. The earliest codex was a single gathering of papyrus pages folded one within the other, a structure often referred to as a quire. It was probably held together with one or two tackets—single stitches made with a thin strip of leather. Today, the most common single-signature structures are referred to as pamphlets or booklets, but these terms don't do justice to their potential. The following three examples illustrate some of the variety that is possible with folded sheets or folios, gathered into a single section or signature and sewn through their folds.

In sewing a single signature, the paper is cut to its final size, folded in half along the spine and pressed with a folder. Each folded sheet is collated with other folios, one inside the other, into a signature of a designated number of pages. Sequencing Folio Pages on page 104 provides additional information.

Nag Hammadi, 2006, 72 pages, 5" × 3¹/₂" (13cm × 9cm)

Two single knots were used to sew *Nag Hammadi*, a 1/4 scale variation of a fourth-century single quire codex. An awl was used to punch two holes for each knot or tacket through the cover, the seventy-two pages (eighteen folios) of mud papyrus and a stay, a small, soft, black leather reinforcement placed in the center of the quire to help keep the thong from damaging the brittle pages. A large needle was threaded with a leather thong and, leaving a tail long enough to tie at the end, the thong was drawn from the outside to the center. The needle was then moved about 1/2" (13mm) to the left, and the leather thong was taken back to the outside of the book where the two ends were tied together and trimmed. The second tacket was sewn in the same way.

law and custom, 2004, 6 pages, 8³/₄" × 11" (22cm × 28cm) closed, 8³/₄" × 22" (22cm × 26cm) open

A knot, a stitch and another knot sewed the single folios into *law and custom*, a bi-fold book with fabric interior. Beginning inside the folded sheet, near the bottom, the black waxed thread, tied with an overhand knot, was passed through to the outside of the black cover and then back through to the inside too, where it was tied off with another overhand knot, cut and secured with a drop of PVA. Two knots appear inside the folio, while one long black stitch is against the black cover. The second folio was sewn in the same way. The two sheets of laser-printed text relate to the discrepancy between law and custom in India, with facts related to the Dowry Prohibition Act (related to bride burning) on the left side, and the Suppression of Immoral Traffic in Women and Girls Act (related to prostitution) on the right.

Materials

Scrap pieces of sturdy board, binders or wood

Ruler

Pencil

Knife, heavy utility

Cutting board

Duct tape, if desired

A piercing cradle is a useful tool to help you align your holes directly along the fold line and pierce them in the same place in each of your signatures. This example, designed to come apart so that it can be easily transported and stored, can be made from three scraps of sturdy board. This cradle was made 10" (25 cm) long by 6½" (17cm) wide, with two legs 4½" (11cm) wide by 2¾" (7cm) tall.

1. Cut a piece of sturdy board for the cradle. It should be long enough for the height of your books and deep enough to support the open signatures. Cut two pieces of sturdy board for the support pieces (legs). The width should be 2" (5cm) less than the width of the cradle, and the height should be about 3" (8cm) for most books.

   With a knife, carefully score down the center length of the cradle board, front and back, without penetrating through the board. Place the cradle facedown, measure 1" (3cm) from the end, center your leg board and draw a line around the thickness of the board. Cut inside the lines with a utility knife to create a slot slightly smaller than the thickness of the leg board. Repeat at the opposite end of the cradle for the remaining leg.

2. Bend the cradle into a V shape, and place the legs inside the slots. Place duct tape along the length of the fold on the bottom if reinforcing seems necessary.

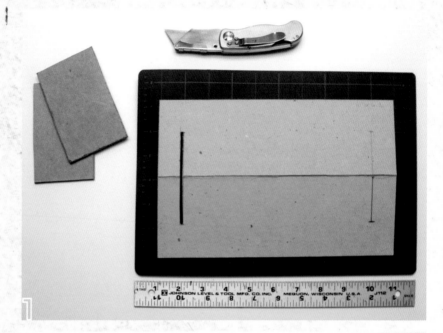

CREATING SIGNATURE AND SPINE TEMPLATES

The first template here is a guide for the accurate placement of a single column of holes for sewing signatures. It can have any number of holes, any distance apart. The second is for accurately placing multiple columns of holes when sewing signatures into the spines of covers. Modify each example to fit your own needs.

1. Cut a sheet of paper the length of the spine, or use an extra book page. Fold the paper in half crosswise to mark the position where the middle hole for sewing will be pierced or punched.

2. Mark approximately 1" (3cm) from the top and 1" (3cm), or slightly more, from the bottom for three holes. Add additional holes by measuring or by folding from each of the outer marks to the middle mark and making new marks at the folds.

3. Fold the template lengthwise to align the marks with the fold of the cradle. Place the opened signature to be pierced snugly against one end of the cradle. Place the template into the center of the signature, being sure that the spines are aligned and straight in the cradle.

4. Hold an awl at right angles to the fold and pierce holes where there are marks, going straight through the template and all pages of the signature.

5. Put an arrow or X in the upper right-hand corner on the template and on each signature to keep the orientation consistent when sewing.

Materials

Signatures

Paper for template

Ruler

Pencil

Awl

Signatures

Piercing cradle

Spines

Paper for template

Clips

Foam core or matboard

Ruler

Pencil

Awl

90° triangle

Cover material

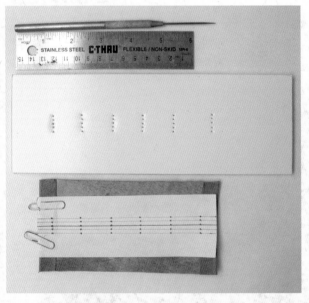

1. Determine the width of the spine template by pressing together the multiple signatures to be bound and measuring the compacted width that they create. Release the signatures and measure the released width of the spine. The width of the template will be halfway between the two measurements. For example, if the width compacted is 1/2" (13mm) and the width released is 1" (3cm), the spine template should be $^3/_4$" (19mm).

2. On a strip of paper the same height as the spine, measure and mark the width of the spine as determined in Step 1. To determine the spacing between the signatures, divide the width of the spine by the number of signatures in the book. Draw parallel lines to indicate where the holes for the signatures will be placed.

3. Position the template used for piercing the signatures along the first line and mark the sewing holes. Repeat the process for each signature. A ruler and 90° triangle can be used as guides for alignment. For example, if you have five signatures and a spine width of $^3/_4$" (19mm), you will have five parallel lines .15" (4mm) apart (.75 / 5). Each line will have the number and placement of sewing holes in your signatures.

4. Clip the template to the spine or cover material. Place the template and material on a scrap of foam core or mat board as support. Using an awl, pierce the holes through the template and material into the support. A ruler and 90° triangle can be used as guides for piercing straight up and down.

5. Put an arrow or X in the upper right-hand corner on the template to match the signatures and keep the orientation consistent when sewing.

SEQUENCING FOLIO PAGES

When you are collating folios into signatures, you need to be aware of the sequence of pages. In this example, there are four folios, for a total of sixteen pages, including the front and back covers. The front and back covers are pages 1 and 16. Inside the cover is page 2 and opposite it, on the same sheet, is page 15 on the inside of the back cover. Making a mock-up is helpful in seeing how the folios will be assembled.

In printing, the process of arranging pages prior to printing is referred to as imposition. (See pages 64–65 for printing on a single sheet.) Some page layout programs can rearrange your single pages for various printing options. For example, "Print Booklet" is one of the "print" choices in the software program InDesign. You can sequence various numbers of pages to make signatures of different sizes. If you are laying out your pages in the computer for printing in an imaging program like Photoshop, you can place images side by side, as shown on page 110.

If you are working with aligning pages that are collaged or painted, you may have to add elements to tie the pages together.

1 folio, four pages							
back	cover	2	15	14	3	4	13
12	5	6	11	10	7	8	9

Four folios (16 pages), sequenced

PAMPHLET AND BUTTERFLY STITCH

Two simple stitches are used for sewing single signatures: the pamphlet stitch and the butterfly stitch.

The pamphlet stitch begins in the center, leaving a tail and passing through to the other side. In a three-hole version, it then goes to one of the outer holes and passes through to the side where the stitching began. Skipping the middle hole, it goes to the opposite hole at the far end, passes through that hole and returns to the center, going back to the side where the beginning tail was left. The two ends are tied together across the middle long stitch with a square knot. The long stitch skipping the middle hole is characteristic of the pamphlet stitch.

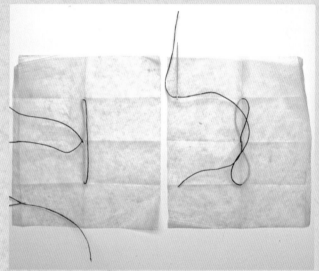

The butterfly stitch is a slight variation. Instead of carrying the thread from the top hole to the bottom hole, you sew back through the center hole, being careful not to split the thread. Go through the bottom hole, make a figure 8, and return to the center. Pass your thread under the first stitch, and tie the ends together. The illustration shows both the pamphlet and butterfly stitches before they have been pulled taunt and tied with a square knot.

Three-Hole Pamphlet and Five-Hole Butterfly Stitch

Shadow Words is made with a three-hole pamphlet stitch. It uses pages of various textures and thicknesses made with gelatin printmaking techniques, collaged lace paper and a handmade rubber stamp. The text is added with inkjet alcohol gel transfers. It has ten folios and a cover of embossed paper slightly larger than the pages, designed to wrap with a 1¼" (3cm) overlap on the fore edge.

Numbers is made with a five-hole butterfly stitch. It is a slight book, a single signature of seven folios, utilizing sheer handmade paper with stenciled numbers made using handmade brass stencils and metal stamps.

Both the pamphlet and butterfly stitch begin in the middle hole of the cover, sewing in and out of each hole in succession. Unlike the three-hole butterfly stitch described previously, the five-hole butterfly stitch makes a figure 8 above the middle hole and another figure 8 below the middle hole. Both of the stitches use the same set of materials.

The differences in the two stitch patterns are noted on the following pages.

Materials

Folios, with or without images and text

Paper cover, if desired

Folder

Ruler

Pencil

Piercing cradle

Template for piercing holes in signatures

Awl

Clamps or paper clips

Needle with an eye large enough to accommodate your thread

Thread, preferably heavy linen

Scissors

Closure, if desired

Shadow Words, 2008, 40 pages 7¼" × 5¼" (18cm × 13cm)

Numbers, 2008, 28 pages 7¾" × 5½" (20cm × 14cm)

Three-Hole Pamphlet Stitch

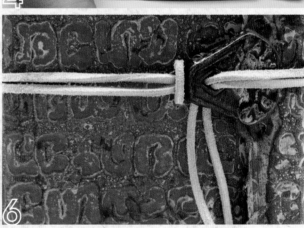

1. Cut folios to their final size, fold each in half and press with a folder. Collate each folio, one inside the other, into a signature and mark the top corner. Add a cover of heavier paper, or use the outer folio as a cover. Align the folios and cover and hold together with clamps or paper clips. Make a template, and pierce the desired number of holes in the signature (see page 103).

2. Pass the needle from the inside middle to the outside, leaving a 3" (8cm) tail. At the top hole, pass the needle from the outside to the inside. Carry the thread to the bottom hole and pass it through to the outside.

3. Being careful not to split the thread, pass the needle through the center hole from the outside to the inside.

4. Make certain that the original tail and the needle are on opposite sides of the long center stitch.

5. Pull the thread taunt, tie the ends in a square knot across the long center stitch and trim excess thread.

6. Make or find an appropriate closure, if desired. For this book, I found the faceplate of an old lock with a hole for a key and three holes for nails or screws. To attach it to the cover wrap, I sewed through the two parallel nail holes with black linen thread. I looped a light-colored leather thong through the remaining nail hole, wrapped the two thongs around the book and slipped them through the keyhole to hold the book closed.

Numbers, 2008, 28 pages, 7³/₄" × 5¹/₂" (20cm × 14cm)

FIVE-HOLE BUTTERFLY STITCH

1. Cut folios to their final size, fold each in half and press with a folder. Collate each folio, one inside the other, into a signature and mark the top corner. Add a cover of heavier paper, or use the outer folio as a cover.

2. Align the folios and cover and hold together with clamps or paper clips.

3. Make a template and pierce the desired number of holes in the signature (see page 103).

4. Pass the needle from the outside middle to the inside, leaving the tail about 3" (8cm) long.

5. Moving toward the top, pass the needle from the inside to the outside at the next hole. At the top hole, pass the needle from the outside to the inside.

6. From the top hole, move down one hole, passing the needle from the inside to the outside, being careful not to split the thread. (This completes the top figure 8.)

7. Go back through the middle hole from outside to inside. Go through the hole next to the bottom from inside to outside. Go through the bottom hole from outside to inside. Go to the next hole up from inside to outside.

8. Finish the second figure 8 by going through the stitch above the middle hole.

9. Pull the thread taunt and tie the ends in a square knot. Trim excess thread, or leave it long as a decorative element.

MULTIPLE-SIGNATURE BOOKS

In advanced codex structures, multiple signatures are attached to form a book "block" by sewing each signature, in succession, to the adjacent signature or to a support that holds the signatures together. If the sewing is to be exposed on the spine, the choice of thread and pattern of sewing will become an integral part of the book. In book blocks where the spine will be covered with paper, fabric or leather, the spine may be smoothed and stabilized with glue and a thin paper with good wet strength.

In these projects, we'll be using a longstitch, a simple in-and-out running stitch that links signatures into the spine, creating a structure that lies flat when open. The sewing is done through holes pierced in the signatures and either holes or slots aligned in the spine. If the signatures have few pages, the rows of stitches will be close together and the spine narrow; if the signatures are fat or you anticipate adding collage elements, the rows of stitching can be spaced farther apart, making a wider spine. When stitching through slots, be careful not to make the slot longer than the semi-compacted width of the signatures, or the stitches will tend to misalign. Directions for creating a template for spines on page 103 will help you make quick and easy longstitch books.

Ideally, a book should be the same thickness at the spine edge and at the fore edge. If either edge is larger, it is referred to as swell. Swell can be caused on the spine edge if the sewing holes are too far apart or if the thread is too thick. In *Mayflower*, this worked to my advantage, as the spine-edge swell

Fasnacht, 2005, 24 pages, 7½" × 6" (20cm × 15cm) (3 folios, 4 signatures)
Fasnacht was made with ephemera gathered during the Basel (Switzerland) Fasnacht celebration, a Protestant carnival similar to Mardi Gras. The multiple signatures were sewn using a longstitch through the black leather cover with red linen thread.

was overcome by adding collage materials to the pages.

For me, swell on the fore edge, caused by added collage materials, is much more common. In purchased blank books, I have often found myself tearing out folios to help retain the shape or, in the case of *India* (see page 45) and *Cuba* (see page 37), having to rebind when I returned home. If you remove pages, do it carefully so that you don't damage the structural integrity of your book.

If you are sewing a longstitch book, you can anticipate fore-edge expansion by spacing your rows of stitches farther apart, sewing with a very heavy thread or sewing in relatively narrow strips of heavy paper the length of the spine to serve as spacers between the folios. If appropriate to your book, consider colored or decorative paper spacers for adding interest while helping to solve a potential problem.

Barcelona, *Wishes*, *Lies*, *Dreams*, *Fasnacht* and *West* are examples of the longstitch sewn through holes punched in leather. In *Fasnacht*, the spine and cover are a single piece of leather, while in *Barcelona*, *Wishes* and *West*, the spine is leather and the covers are other materials. These structures are especially nice to work in when you travel since you can sew several signatures into a piece of leather long enough to accommodate additional signatures if needed, and trim it to a final size when the signatures are completed. *One Life* is a keyhole variation.

In the following projects, we'll use the longstitch to sew through a leather spine and through a full leather cover.

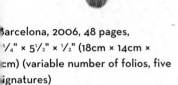

Barcelona, 2006, 48 pages, 7¼" × 5½" × ½" (18cm × 14cm × cm) (variable number of folios, five ignatures)

Barcelona is an example of a longstitch ook sewn through slots that was made n a workshop with Keith Smith. The five ignatures are sewn with tan linen thread a staggered stitch pattern over the ead and tail through eight slots cut into red kangaroo leather spine. The cover is lack paper over board.

One Life, 2003, 43 pages, 5¾" × 4½" (15cm × 11cm) (four folios, seven signatures)

The spine of *One Life* is made of black bookcloth with a section in the middle cut in an X shape and glued open to create a "keyhole." The natural linen stitches go over the black book cloth at the head and tail and into the black, beige and white signatures that are revealed in the open space at the middle of the spine. Black ribbon covers the transition and finishes the spine. Glued onto the natural linen cover is an antique glass photographic plate. (See pages from the book on page 37.)

West 2005 24 pages, 7½" × 6¾" (20cm × 17cm) (four folios, three signatures)

West was made in Santa Fe, New Mexico, while I was teaching a workshop for Arches. The signatures of Canson Mi-Teintes and acrylic paste paper were completed with collage, graphite, colored pencil and copper foil. The cover is patinaed copper and leather. The signatures are attached with an exposed longstitch. Because the stitching seemed too light for the heavy leather and metal, I wove crosswise between the vertical stitches with a heavy cord and added a single found earring. The title was added with rubber-stamp letters, clear ink and embossing powder. (See pages from the book on page 17.)

Wishes, Lies, Dreams, 1999, 120 pages, 4" × 3½" (10cm × 9cm) (five folios, six signatures)

Wishes, Lies, Dreams is a small, fat book with six signatures of five folios each. It is sewn together with a longstitch through four holes in a heavy brown leather spine attached to pieces of sheet metal. The stitching, using dark green cord, begins with an overhand knot about 2" (5cm) from the end of the cord, leaving a piece hanging at the bottom. Instead of going over the head and the tail of the book, this stitching pattern goes in and out up the spine, then across to the next signature on the surface of the leather so that there is a combination of vertical and horizontal stitches. The final stitch is tied with an overhand knot and a piece of cord left hanging. Metal beads are attached to the ends with knots and glue. The same cord is used for a tie that wraps around a metal closure. The title was added with punched letters rubbed with black paint.

LONGSTITCH BOOK WITH A LEATHER SPINE

Materials

Folios, with or without images and text, assembled into signatures

Leather for a spine

Spine lining material: nonwoven fabric, Tyvek or paper

Ruler

Pencil

Folder

Glue or adhesive as needed

Glue brush

Snap-blade or X-Acto knife

Cutting board

Clamps or paper clips

Piercing cradle

Template for piercing holes in signatures

Template for piercing holes in cover

Scrap of foam core or mat board

Awl

Needle with an eye large enough to accommodate your thread

Thread, preferably heavy linen

Scissors

In this project, we're using papers that were aged in chapter one to complete the book block for *Mayflower;* in the following chapter, we'll make a cover for the book. To assemble my signatures and incorporate images and text, I began by using a template to cut all of the pieces of aged paper and white-washed documents and maps into consistent folios 5¾" × 11½" (15cm × 29cm).

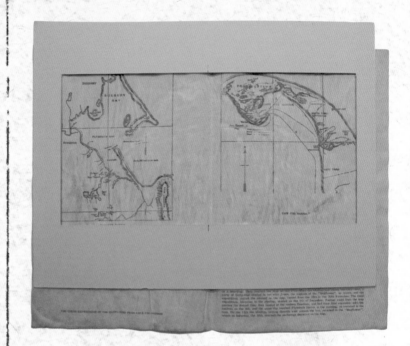

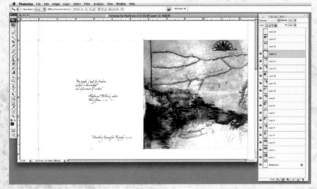

In Photoshop, I made all my photographs 5¾" × 5¾" (15cm × 15cm) to cover each page full-bleed. I toned and textured the images, and then began the process of sequencing the pages. I made a Photoshop template the size of the folio, decided which images would be printed and added them to the layout. You can see all of the individual images in the layers on the right side of the screen. The screenshot of the template layout shows the first and last page of the final signature (see page 21).

On a sheet of 13" × 20" (33cm × 51cm) carrier paper, I printed a gray outline exactly the size of my folio. I used double-stick tape across the top edge to hold the textured folios in place. The photograph shows the images that appear on page 2 and 11 coming off the printer. The textured paper works well with the images.

There are lists of passengers, supplies, maps and my handwritten words and phrases throughout, but the primary text used in the book is a Nathaniel Philbrick quotation: "One people's quest for freedom resulted in the conquest and enslavement of another."

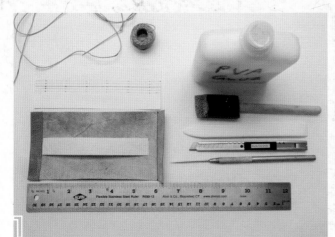

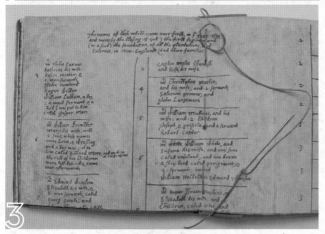

1. Make a template and pierce holes in the signatures (see page 103). Cut a piece of leather the width of the spine plus 2" (5cm) and the height of the signatures plus 1" (3cm). Mark the head and tail turn-ins at slightly less than $\frac{1}{2}$" (13mm) and score the mark with a folder. Coat the turn-ins with glue. Fold along the score on the turn-ins and press with a folder. Cut lining material the width of the spine and the length minus the turn-ins. Center the lining and glue it to the leather. While many spines don't need lining, soft materials and leathers that can easily stretch benefit from being reinforced.

2. Make a template and pierce holes in the leather spine (see page 103). Measure one length of thread the height of each signature plus an additional length. Begin inside the first signature at the bottom hole, leaving a 3" (8cm) tail. Sew around the tail of the signature and tie a square knot to secure the thread.

Continue to the next hole inside the signature. Pass the thread to the outside. Continue sewing in and out the holes until the head on the outside is reached. Come over the head and add a second signature. Pass the needle into the inside top hole of the second signature.

3. Pass the needle to the outside and continue in and out, adding signatures alternately at the head and tail, until the end of the last signature is reached.

Go around the head and make an overhand knot into the last stitch to secure the sewing. The staggered stitch pattern in Mayflower's spine shows five signatures each with six sets of holes spaced $\frac{1}{2}$" (13mm) from the head and tail and .15" (4mm) apart.

Mayflower, book block to be covered. (See pages 124–125.)

Materials

Folios, with or without images and text, assembled into signatures

Material for a cover

Snap-blade or craft knife

Cutting board

Ruler

90° triangle

Pencil

Piercing cradle

Template for piercing holes in signatures

Template for piercing holes in cover

Awl

Scrap of foam core or mat board

Glue or adhesive as needed

Glue brush

Needle with an eye large enough to accommodate your thread

Thread, preferably heavy linen

Scissors

Cord or ribbon as a decorative element or tie, if desired

On a trip to Cuzco, Machu Picchu and the Sacred Valley in Peru, I gathered ephemera related to the culture, history and current events of the area. I worked in two pamphlet-sewn signatures I had carried with me. When I got home, I chose a piece of leather for the cover, untied the two signatures, added holes and used a longstitch to sew them into the cover.

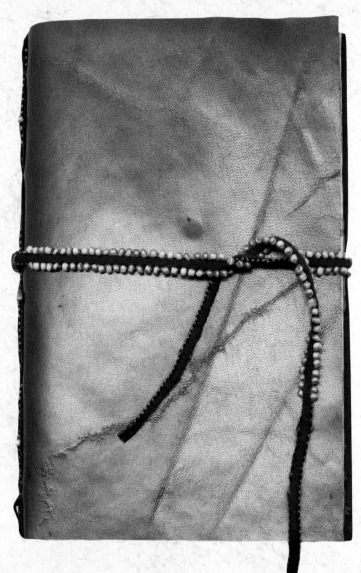

Land of the Inca, 2008, 48 pages, 8" × 5¼" (20cm × 13cm)

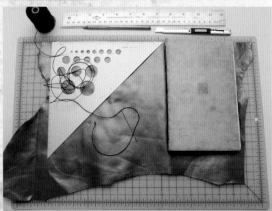

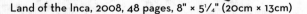

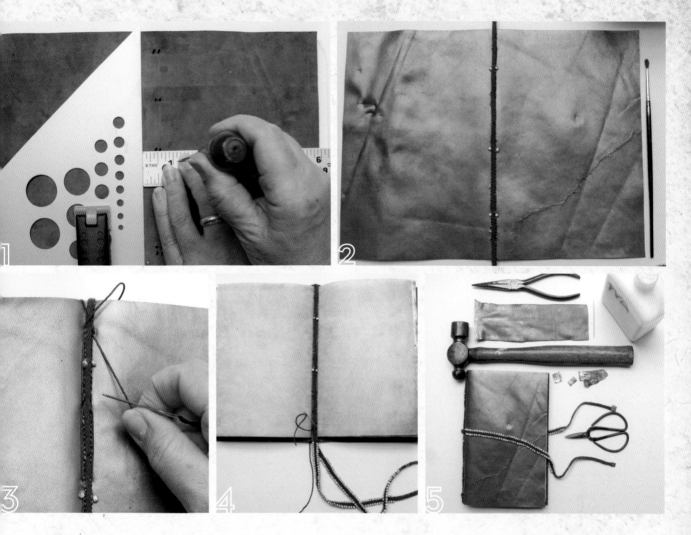

1. Make a template and pierce holes in signatures (see page 103), then make a spine template and pierce holes in the cover (see page 103). I measured and marked my leather cover on the inside.

2. Measure one length of thread the height of the spine times the number of signatures plus one additional length. Beginning at the first bottom hole on the outside of the cover, leave a 3" (8cm) tail and pass the needle through to the inside. Go in and out until the needle is on the outside of the top hole. Stitch horizontally across to the second set of holes. Pass your needle through to the inside of the second signature. Go in and out, repeating the steps, until the needle is on the outside of the last hole. Tie your thread and cut off the excess.

   Because *Land of the Inca* has only two signatures and six holes, I decided to give the spine more interest by incorporating a length of woven cord from Peru. I put PVA between the spine holes and glued the cord in place.

3. I'm essentially outlining the cord with thread, going over the head, through the inside top hole into the second signature and returning to the bottom, but instead of tying off, I'm going around the tail and sewing up and down the spine to fill in the alternate stitches so that the thread on both sides will appear continuous.

   The second time around, I positioned the cord so that the stitches at the head would form an X. When I returned to the beginning, I tied off the threads with a square knot.

4. Since the cord was long enough to carry into the center of the book, I glued it into the gutter between the two signatures, sewed it in place, trimmed and glued both ends and tied an X over the ends to make the bottom of the spine match the top.

5. If desired, add a tie of cord, ribbon, raffia, string or other material. I overlapped my two remaining pieces of cord and sewed them together to make a tie. To cover the sewing and make it more secure, I hammered a small piece of lead, wrapped it around the sewing on the spine and squeezed it with needle-nose pliers. I secured it to the spine with PVA and sewing. I also made lead crimps around the ends of the cords to keep them from raveling.

- Create more complex stitching patterns. Place your holes in varying arrangements, some closer together and others farther apart, or some closer to the spine and others deeper into the cover. Also consider stitching back into some holes more than once.

- If you're doing a more complex stitching pattern, use more than one color of thread.

- Make a collection of various colors and weights of thread, twine, ribbon and leather thongs so you will always have options. Use more than one if they work well together.

- Folded, adhesive-bound and sewn bindings can be combined in various ways. For example, pamphlets can be sewn into the depths of concertina folds or onto their outer points. In *Vietnam Journal* (see page 6) and *Goin Home* (see page 118), each single sheet is glued in succession with a wide band of adhesive. They each have soft front covers and two-piece hinged back covers that function as if they were side-sewn. Consider ways you can combine structures to create books that work for you.

- Begin a collection of beads, charms or other decorative elements you can add to the ends of your threads if you begin your stitching on the outside of your book.

- As you work don't hesitate to change your original plan if a better idea emerges. Figure it out as you go.

- In a signature each folio can be a different color, weight and texture. Just make sure there is a good flow and it all works well together.

- When planning the pages for a side-sewn book, measure the width from the spine edge needed for the fastening device, and don't put text or important content in that area. A post and screw will take considerably more space than thread. If working with paper, don't place your holes so close to the spine that it might tear.

- Inexpensive dental floss threaders can be purchased at a local drugstore.

- If you need to have your knot close to the beginning or ending of a stitch, put an awl through the loop of the thread and hold it tight against the point where you want the knot. As you tighten your thread, it will slide against the awl.

- When deciding how far apart the holes will be placed, how far in they will be from the spine edge and how large in diameter they need to be, consider the thickness of the thread or sewing material and the size of the book.

- To keep the fore edges of the pages at the same level, most signatures are made up of three or four folios (twelve or sixteen pages). However, your signatures can be made of whatever number of folios you choose.

- Because a quire is usually rather fat, the folios may give the appearance of decreasing in width since, as they are added to the outside signature, the increasing thickness of the spine makes them fan outward. You have three options: you can decide you like this shape, you can add progressively longer folios to the quire to make the fore edge square, or, if there is no content that would be damaged, you can trim the folios so that the fore-edge is square.

- You may use whatever number of holes you want, but an uneven number will allow the sewing pattern to begin and end at the same place to be tied off.

- You can begin your sewing on the inside or the outside of your signature. If you begin and end on the outside, you can make your tied ends a feature with added beads and decorative elements.

- You can make an awl by putting a strong, sharp needle into a craft knife handle.

- Be careful to keep your awl or piercing needle straight up and down, perpendicular to the pages. Piercing at an angle will create holes that misalign the pages when sewn.

- Holes too close to the head and tail may weaken the paper and cause it to tear. Holes too far away won't provide adequate support. A half inch to an inch usually works well.

- As a less elegant substitute for sewing, a long-necked saddle-stitch stapler or an office stapler, opened flat, may be used to insert staples into a signatures spine.

- Punching holes in some fabric causes the threads to fray. Using leather, a nonwoven fabric, polyester (ultra) suede or felt avoids the problem of fraying.

- When joining signatures, it is often useful to have your needle bent very slightly. Hold each end of a straight needle with a pair of pliers, place it against a hot plate or tacking iron and bend gently.

- If you don't want your stitching exposed, you can cover the spine with paper, fabric or leather. You can also add a spine liner, as in *Mayflower,* or, if you prefer a hard spine, you can sew through a strip of board.

Opposite and above: Sicily, 2008, 56 pages, 8" × 7" (20cm x 18cm) red kangaroo binding with gold leaf, images collaged in Sicily into a pre-made blank book

COVERS, BOXES AND UNBOUND COLLECTIONS

Up to this point, there has been a lot of focus on a book's interior, including much discussion about individual pages, folios and signatures. Because we've already made several covers throughout this book, the placement of this chapter may make the topic seem like icing on the cake. Don't be tempted to treat the cover of your book as an afterthought. It is the first thing that the viewer encounters, and therefore gives an indication of the intent and of the content of the book by virtue of its weight, color, texture and how it feels. It defines the book's form.

After exploring some of the options available for covers, we'll go beyond what's thought of as typical book form and look at unbound collections, boxes and book forms that become sculptural. Be open to interesting objects; look past their original use to consider how they might be transformed. And, although I am most likely to use found objects in my work, use whatever skills you have to make boxes and sculptural forms to express your concepts.

Common Ground, 2008, 60 pages, 7³/₄" × 6" (20cm × 15cm) a painted and laser-engraved wood cover and leather spine sewn over tapes (Pages from the book can be seen on page 26)

As an artist-in-residence at Universal Laser Systems in Phoenix, I engraved into painted and unpainted wood, leather, glass, acrylic mirror, Plexiglas, fabric, painted metal, lead and marble. Laser is a fascinating tool with great creative potential.

COVERS

Mass-produced books are typically categorized as either softcover or hardcover. A softcover book is described as having a cover made of flexible cardboard or paper that is glued directly onto the spine, and a hardcover book is made of two cover boards of inflexible material separated by a spine. But those categorizations blur completely when you attempt to apply them to artist books. We'll be looking at soft and hard covers made from a wide range of materials, and at a simple way of attaching them to a book block.

The simplest kinds of covers are created in two or three pieces then attached to the book. This allows for an almost infinite choice of cover materials, including found objects, wood, clay, polymer clay, heavy leather, copper and binder's board. If desired, the boards and spines can be covered and decorated with leather, cloth, paper (Unryu is especially forgiving) or metal foil before being attached.

Some of the possibilities for future covers that I have found or made include a plaster "head-

stone," the printing block for a game board, small wooden cutting boards, a wooden bookend with a small metal image of Pegasus, dove-tailed boards, square metal pieces, a carved woodblock for printing, a cast resin plaque resembling ivory, a black painted clay square with the title "witch" embossed into it and two polymer clay covers wrapped over wood with objects embedded.

In a couple of demonstrations coming up, the back and front covers are made independently from the book block, then attached. In the first demonstration, the fabric-covered boards are attached to an accordion book that has no spine. In the second demonstration, a leather spine is glued to a drumleaf structure, and printed copper foil over wood covers are glued to the first and last folio pages, which serve as endpapers.

In the third demonstration, a leather cover, incorporating an inset tile, is glued to a book block of signatures sewn through a leather spine.

Goin Home, 1999, 52 pages, 7" × 6¼" (18cm × 16cm)
After being away for a number of years, I returned to the area of my childhood, the Gulf Coast of Alabama, Mississippi and Louisiana. The book I collaged while visiting was a commercial blank book, similar to *Vietnam Journal* (see page 6). The paper cover was wrapped with a vintage quilt piece. A closure was made from a metal ornament with an image detail glued into the circular section above the gargoyle head. The ornament was glued to extend beyond the flap, a metal plate was glued to the front cover under the ornament overlap, and a magnet strip was attached to the back of the ornament to hold the cover closed. The title was written with silver marker.

Magdalene Laundries, 2003, 72 pages, 6" × 4¹/₂" (15cm × 11cm) (See more images on pages 22·23 and another view of cover page)

The book used for *Magdalene Laundries* has a binding in the late Coptic style, which was made in a workshop with Shanna Leino. Historically accurate in structure, the boards were made with layers of laminated papyrus that were wrapped with black leather for the cover. Working from a drawing I made, the decoration for both the front and back covers was completed before the leather was attached to the book. It included blind tooling the drawing into the leather with a folder, sections cut or punched out to expose red leather glued underneath, stitching with red thread and a small square of gold leaf. A loop of leather thong was secured in the back cover to wrap around a handmade brass peg held into the front cover with a rivet.

Solar Cross, 2007, 28 pages, 13³/₄" × 13¹/₄" (35cm × 34cm)

An inkjet print over a collage constructed of gold moiré film, aluminum foil tape and silver leaf glued to precoated aluminum became the cover for *Solar Cross.* The printed cover was adhered with a sheet of MACtac clear adhesive to the paper cover of a book originally made in a workshop with Suzanne Moore. (See page 91.) A spine of crumpled, sanded aluminum foil tape was added to cover the aluminum edges. Black oil paint was rubbed into the creases and abrasions to tone the silver.

Making and Attaching Independent Covers

Materials

Book block

Boards to be covered

Material to cover boards

Pencil

Snap-blade or craft knife

Cutting board

Ruler or straightedge

Scissors

Glue or adhesive as needed

Glue brush

Folder

Paper, waxed

Paper, scrap or other clean waste paper

Weight

Chopping mats or other nonabsorbent hard surface

A concertina book is featured in this demo, and this type of binding is typically left without a spine so that it can expand and stand for viewing.

Paper-backed fabric designed for bookmaking is ideal for inkjet printing, but you can also choose other fabric for printing—it just needs to be ironed to a stiff backing, such as freezer paper, first.

Steps A1, A2 and A3 show additional alternative steps. I wrapped a piece of badly worn antique fabric as a second layer around a set of covers in the same olive green book cloth. I inkjet printed the title, "Viewpoint," onto the antique fabric.

 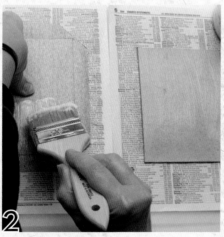 

1. To prepare your paper for covering the first board, place the board on the cover material and trace around it, adding a 1" (3cm) margin to be the turn-in (the portion that is wrapped around) on each side. Trim the excess cover material.

Set the board against each corner and, using the board's thickness as a guide, draw a diagonal line across the corners.

2. Trim the corner triangles away to remove bulk. Coat the back of the cover material and the front of the board with glue, covering the edges completely.

3. Place the board on the cover material. Wrap the turn-ins of two opposite edges around to the back of the board and smooth. Crimp the allowance that had been left to cover the corners and burnish with a folder. Repeat the process for the remaining two edges and for the other cover.

4. Instead of just wrapping the cover material turn-ins around with your fingers, you can lift the edge of the cover that is away from you and roll it forward on the edge remaining on the table to achieve a smooth turn-in.

5. To attach the covers to the book block, orient the front, back, top and bottom of the book and have the covers oriented to match. Place a sheet of scrap paper under the first page of the book, and apply a coat of glue on the outside front of the book block.

6. Align the book block with the cover so that the margins are visible, and carefully press it onto the cover. Repeat the steps with the last page and the back cover. Press under weight until dry.

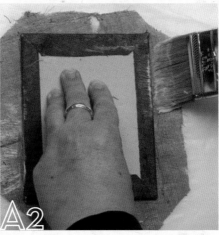

A1. Because my fabric in this alternative process is thin and delicate with tears and holes, I'm gluing it over a set of boards, as prepared in Steps 1–4. I coated the board with a heavy layer of gel medium.

A2. I repeated the wrapping process by gluing the printed fabric onto the pre-wrapped board.

A3. Instead of rolling the board forward, as described in the previous demonstration to achieve the smooth turn-in of the flap, you can use waxed paper as your scrap paper and pull it around the board edge to push the fabric margin smoothly onto the back of the cover.

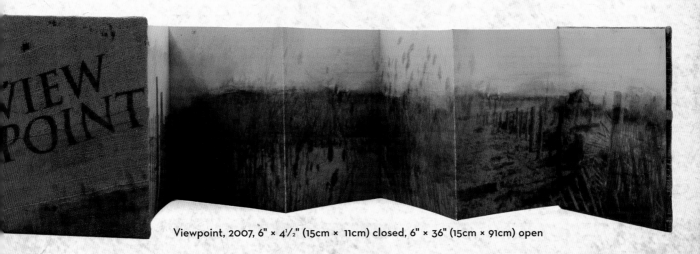

Viewpoint, 2007, 6" × 4½" (15cm × 11cm) closed, 6" × 36" (15cm × 91cm) open

FOIL OVER WOOD

Materials

Book block

Boards to be covered

Material to cover boards (foil)

Glue or adhesive as needed

Glue brush

Folder

Material for spine

Oil pastels, pigment or paint to color leather

Weight

Optional: digital file of cover, computer, imaging software, inkjet printer, white paper for carrier sheet if needed, inkjet precoat and a brush for applying precoat

A spine is included in this demo, though just like the cover in the previous demo, the pieces are covered independently. The spine is attached to the book block, and the covers attached to the spine. The spine wrap can also be a design element that not only hides parts of the binding, but also protects the back of the book.

The cover for *Climate Change* uses inkjet-printed copper foil over wood and a leather spine, but you could use heavy aluminum foil and fabric. (If your printer has "pizza wheels" that track on nonporous surfaces, reread the information on page 11.) Any heavy board would be suitable, but model airplane plywood is becoming one of my favorite boards for its lightweight strength and ease of use. The images for this project were created on pages 28–29 and the book block constructed on pages 86–87.

Climate Change, 2007, 24 pages, 7" × 5½"
(18cm × 14cm)

climate change

1. Design the cover on paper or make the cover image in the computer. This image, a medium gray silhouette, was designed to allow the copper to show through and extended to carry onto the wrapped edges. The cut lines, shown in red, were printed on a paper template but not on the copper.

2. Apply two coats of precoat to the foil, allowing each coat to dry thoroughly, and brushing one coat in one direction and the second coat in a perpendicular direction. Tape the copper to a piece of carrier paper and print the cover design with an inkjet printer onto the precoated foil.

3. Attach the foil to your cover boards in the same manner as the fabric on pages 120–121. If your foil happens to be adhesive-backed material, you won't need to add glue. Leave an allowance for wrapping the corners by measuring with the thickness of the board as described in Step 1 on page 120. Because I wanted the copper to really cover well, I made a pattern with an extra extension for wrapping around the side of the corner and used it for cutting all four corners.

4. Cut a piece of leather, paper or fabric 1" (3cm) taller and 1" (3cm) wider than the book block spine. Score 1/2" (13mm) turn-ins at the head and tail edges of the spine material with a folder. Brush glue over the turn-ins on the back of the material and fold them flat, pressing with a folder. Brush glue on the back of the spine material and on the spine of the book block. Center the spine material over the spine of the book block, wrapping the excess over onto the book block, and burnish everything well.

5. Following Steps 5 and 6 on page 121, apply a coat of glue on the outside front of the book block. Align the book block with the cover so that the margins are visible, and carefully press the book block onto the cover.

LEATHER COVER WITH INSET

Book block with attached spine
material

Item to insert

Boards to be covered

Material to cover boards

Cutting board

Ruler

Pencil or pen

90° triangle

Snap-blade or craft knife

Paper, scrap

Paper, waxed

Vinyl spackle

Spreaders, credit cards or pieces
of plastic

Piece of nonwoven fabric or paper
for filler

Wheat paste

Paste brush

Glue or other adhesive

Glue brushes, small and large

Scissors

Folder

Paper for covering the inside of
the covers

Chopping mats or other nonabsorbent hard surfaces

Weight

Having aged the paper on page 21 and sewn the book signatures into a leather spine on pages 110–111, we're ready to make a cover for *Mayflower* and attach it to the spine. Except for being covered with leather and having an inset, this three-piece cover is made using the same techniques as the previous cover. Because there is a thick glazed tile to be incorporated into the front cover, I'm using a piece of Gatorfoam, a dimensionally stable archival board, about the same thickness as the tile, but binder's board, wood or plywood cut to size and sanded are also good choices. Glue works well with most materials, but it can stain leather; wheat paste is preferred.

Mayflower, 2008, 60 pages, 6" × 6" × 1½" (15cm × 15cm × 4cm) leather over Gatorfoam with glazed tile inset

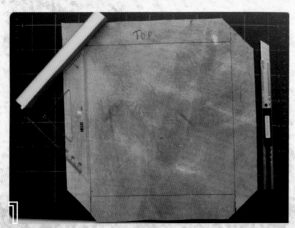

1. Cut the cover material as described in Step 1 on page 120. A 90° triangle parallel to the traced edge of the board will help to draw a perfect diagonal line across the corner of the cover material for the board corner allowance. Note the space left for the thickness of the Gatorfoam board.

2. Position the item to be incorporated on the cover material and trace around it. Make several cuts from the center to the traced edges. Coat the back of the cut edges with wheat paste, turn them under and press them in place with a folder. Position the cut material on the cover board and use the hole as a template for tracing on the board. Cut the hole in the board deep enough to accommodate the item and place the item into the hole, with glue if needed.

Because my shape was square and centered on the cover, it was easy to position and trace around. I cut an X from corner to corner across the center of the traced shape to open the leather. Instead of cutting and turning under the edges, you may want to stretch the cover material into the space if your item is relatively shallow. Wheat paste rubbed into leather helps it to stretch well.

Coat the entire back of the cover material with wheat paste. Place the cover material on the board, around the embedded item, wrap the board edges with the excess material and press into place with a folder.

3. Fill any gaps on the back of the front cover with vinyl spackle and let dry.

4. Wrap the board for the back cover. Fill the indentation created by the wrapped leather edges on both covers with a material the thickness of the leather and glue in place, using PVA or gel medium. (PVA is a medium wetter than gel and will go into the fibers of heavy fabric, if that is what you are using to even out the surface.)

5. On your pre-made book block, trim the edges of the spine material on a diagonal at the head and tail of the book block so that they won't be seen when the covers are attached. With scrap paper under the trimmed spine material, coat with glue. Press the appropriate cover against the glued spine material. Repeat with the remaining cover. Because this cover is glued only to the spine material, the process is slightly different than the previous examples. I'm using the book block made on pages 110–111.

6. Cut two pieces of paper, slightly smaller than the book covers, and coat them with glue. Press one against the inside front cover and the other against the inside back cover. Place waxed paper between the book block and the cover. Place the book between two chopping mats and press under weight until dry.

The brown handmade paper I chose for the inside covers is similar in color and texture to my leather.

BOXES

Found boxes come in all shapes, sizes and materials, and they may or may not initially resemble books in their appearance or function. They may be open or have lids that are removable or attached. They may immediately suggest a topic, such as the Lucky Strike cigarette boxes I bought to make a book related to my parents, who both smoked "Luckies" and died of smoking-related illnesses.

During an artist-in-residency at Harvard Medical School's Countway Library, I produced a series of work called *Ars Longa—Vita Brevis*. It incorporates photographs of the library's anatomical specimens, medical artifacts, rare books and manuscripts. The work produced was as widely varied as the source material and included several boxes and book-like forms, including *Tabula* and *Braun Box*.

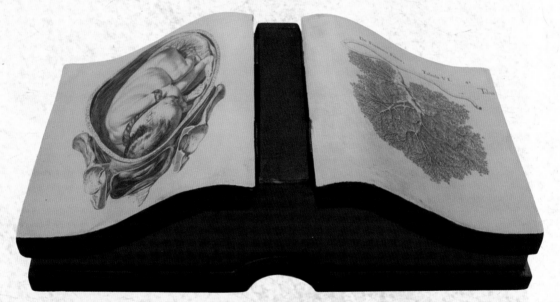

Tabula, 2006, 7¼" × 13¾" × 4¼" (18cm × 35cm × 11cm) inkjet print on shaped wood box

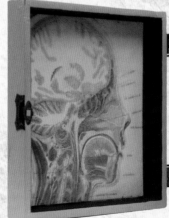
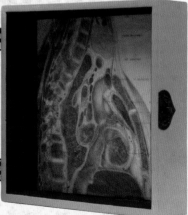

Braun Box, 2006, 7¼" × 7¼" × 2¾" (18cm × 18cm × 7cm) inkjet print with encaustic

Reserve, 2004, 14" × 11" × 1" (36cm × 28cm × 3cm)

Reserve is a wall-hanging box that contains a miniature book version of two murals I produced for the Federal Reserve Bank of Boston. The Articles of Confederation, which authorizes the federal banking system, provides the background for a wooden pedestal with a brass eagle, on which the book is placed.

Las Mourtas de Juarez, 2007,
14" × 4¼" × 2" (36cm × 11cm × 5cm)

Since 1993, there have been hundreds of unsolved homicides in Ciudad Juarez, Mexico, across the border from El Paso, Texas. Most have been young women, age fifteen to twenty-two, who are workers in Juarez factories. This carved wooden "santos," traditional to Mexico, holds a wooden book, to which I added an accordion fold commemorating the loss.

Incendiary Devices, 2008, five pieces of variable sizes, approximately 6" × 6" (15cm × 15cm) each

After an Independence Day celebration, I found a group of empty fireworks casings on the beach. Because they share a similar history and technology with military rockets and other explosives, I used them to house discriminatory, insulting and hostile words. The words, which may be the most incendiary and inflammatory of devices, were written, printed or made with a label maker on acetate, paper or pencils and placed on or into the empty paper casings.

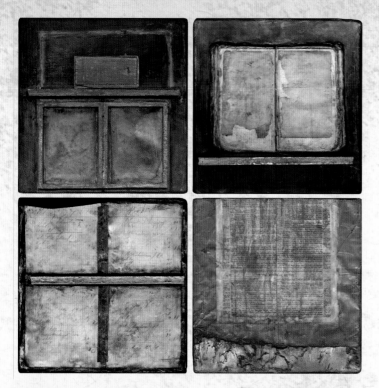

Boxed in, Ledger, Indebted and Book of Ruth, 4 of 48 from the series

Sacred and Mundane, 2001, 12" × 12" (30cm × 30cm) each

Hung in a quilt-like grid at the Art Complex Museum, these pieces use the humblest of materials—plaster, tar and wax—to transform the discarded bits and pieces of a woman's life into intimate and powerful collages.

GulfCoast, 2005, 3 pages, 14½" × 9½" × 3½" (37cm × 24cm × 9cm) closed, 14½" × 19" × 2½" (37cm × 48cm × 6cm) open

In 2005, Hurricane Katrina's devastation of the Gulf Coast, where grew up, was in my thoughts as I created this portable bifold "altar Constructed in a black painted wooden box originally used to house chemistry set, it was deep enough to accommodate items more three dimensional than usually found in books.

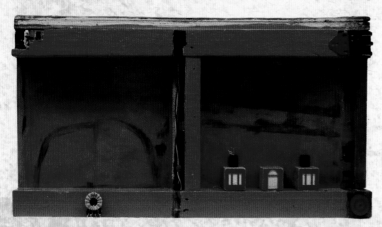

SafeHouse, 2006, 12" × 22¾" × 2" (30cm × 58cm × 5cm)

In 2006, thinking of terrorist attacks, I constructed SafeHouse from a discarded piece of wood shelving, children's toys and electrical components.

Ideally, you should plan your book in advance, including how you will handle your closures and titles. Rarely am I so thoughtful. For me, everything tends to evolve, and components are added as I find them or need them. But paying attention to these important details can add much to the overall success of your book.

Shown here are details from sixteen of the books we have discussed. Reading left to right, top to bottom they are:

Shadow Words (page 105), *Bingo* (page 67), *Patriot Act* (page 55), *Sicily* (page 115)
Nag Hammadi (page 15), *Barcelona* (page 109), *Goin Home* (page 118), *Vietnam Journal* (page 6)
Fasnacht (page 108), *Cuba* (page 37), *9/11 + 5* (page 84), *timeXposure* (page 95)
Promised Land (page 44), *failed rose* (page 82), *Copper* (page 34), *West* (page 109)

Creating a See-Through Box

Materials

Hinged folding picture frame with glass and backing removed

Plexiglas or other lightweight plastic

Transparent or translucent images

Ruler

Plastic scoring tool or snap-blade knife

Cutting board

Straightedge

Clamps

Glue or adhesive as needed

Heavy-bodied clear adhesive like E-6000 or Goop

Weight

Light passing through two or more transparent or translucent images creates a relationship between the images. If they are separated by a space, the relationship is less defined and the edges may blur or shift with movement. You can create an intriguing visual experience by choosing related or contrasting images or text.

For this project, you will want a hinged picture frame, with the outside as attractive as the inside, and four pieces of clear plastic to replace the glass and backing material. Translucent or transparent images will be layered and glued to the plastic to create the front cover, inside front and back pages and back cover.

Sacred Megaliths, 2007, 11" × 18" (28cm × 46cm) open, 11" × 9" × 2½" (28cm × 46cm × 6cm) closed

Stonehenge, with light passing through

I found a print, "Stonehenge," from a 1999 series called "timeXposure." It was laminated to a translucent plastic lenticular lens, and it was large enough to yield four pieces for this project.

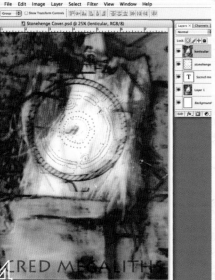

1. Find or make four or more transparent or translucent images for the cover, back and two inside pages. Place the images between two layers of plastic for the front cover and first page. Be sure that the images work together when viewed from both sides, and that the light can continue to pass through.

   Measure each opening carefully, or use the glass from the frame as a template. Draw around the template on the four pieces of plastic. My frame had thin wood spacers that I used for measuring.

2. Place the plastic on a cutting mat. Place a straightedge along the cutting line and clamp it to the edge of the table. Score the plastic with many shallow cuts using a plastic scoring tool. Since my image was already glued to the plastic, I cut both image and plastic at the same time.

3. Align the score of the plastic with the edge of the table. Hold the piece flat on the table, and push down against the piece that extends off the table edge until it breaks away. Cut through any paper backing that may be on the plastic. Repeat the process for the remaining pieces.

4. To determine the best font, size and placement for a title, I scanned the cover into Photoshop and fit a diagram of the Stonehenge site plan into the circle.

5. Use adhesive laminate in clear sheets to invisibly glue transparent images to the plastic, or use other adhesives or tape if they are not visible or don't detract. Make sure none of the components will move or fall out from between the layers of plastic. Repeat the process for the second page and back cover.

The title and diagram were printed on transparent film, sprayed with Scotch Super 77, pressed against the plastic and put under pressure to dry. Since my images were translucent, the slight spray pattern of the glue wasn't noticeable.

6. Check the glued pieces to be sure that they fit into the frame properly. On the back of the plastic, place a thin line of heavy-bodied clear adhesive around the outer edges. Keep the glue within the margin that will be covered by the frame edge.

   Place the pieces into the frame, press firmly into place and dry under weight, if needed.

UNBOUND COLLECTIONS

Unbound books are often collections of materials that, for various reasons, shouldn't be bound. We'll look at a number of examples of unbound books, and I'm sure you can think of many other collections that can be contained within wrappings, boxes or portfolios. The pieces within the collection may be the same size and shape, or they may be a totally varied group of items. Occasionally, collections come in packaging that make suitable containers, but there are times when you need to find a way of holding a group of objects together.

In 1997, I completed a series of images called *Ennobling the Ordinary*. Some years later, I printed miniature versions of the images and glued them to small pieces of wood. Finding them on my bookshelf, I decided to make a housing for them. Instead of just dropping them into a bag or box, I decided on a wrapped pouch with pockets to hold each board, similar to a wrap for silverware or jewelry.

The collection was placed along the horizontal center of a piece of leather. The bottom edge was turned up, and pockets were sewn into the leather. A flap was left on the top to fold over and enclose the collection. A leather thong was sewn to the wrap with a loop at one end to slip over a bead and act as a closure.

The finished piece has the feel of something that might have held precious objects in the Middle Ages.

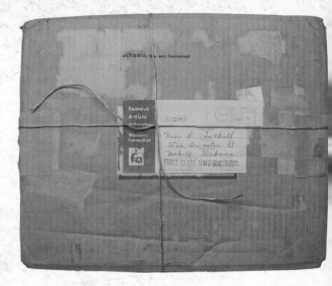

Famous Artist, 1955–2008, 40 pages in box 12³/₈" × 15¹/₈" × 1" (31cm × 38cm × 3cm)

Famous Artist houses a collection of nine mail-order lessons I completed as a fifteen-year-old student of the Famous Artist School. It is housed in the corrugated cardboard box that was sent back and forth with lessons completed and corrected with tissue overlays.

Ennobling the Ordinary, 2008, 6 wood images 2³/₄" × 1⁵/₈" (7cm × 4cm) in wrapped pouch 3" × 2³/₄" × 1³/₄" (8cm × 7cm × 4cm) closed, 6¹/₄" × 19³/₄" (16cm × 50cm) open

Terme, 2006, 12 pieces 6½" × 4" (17cm × 10cm) each in a printed paper wrapper

Terme began with a copper printing plate of the baths (terme) of Caracalla. From a small book on the ancient terme of Rome, found in a street vendor's bookstall, I took a map of locations of all the baths and drawings and diagrams of Caracalla's baths. At the Capitoline Museum, I found reproduction coins of the heads of some of the emperors who had built baths, including Nero and Constantine, which completed the book. The individual collages were wrapped in the paper showing the print of the copper plate.

Rations, 2008, 9 books 4¼" × 5¾" (11cm × 15cm) each in a case 5¼" × 6¾" (13cm × 17cm)

Rations is a leather folder holding War Ration Books issued in the 1940s by the U.S. Office of Price Administration to ensure the "right to buy your fair share of certain goods made scarce by war." Comments related to our conspicuous consumption and resulting obesity problems have been added.

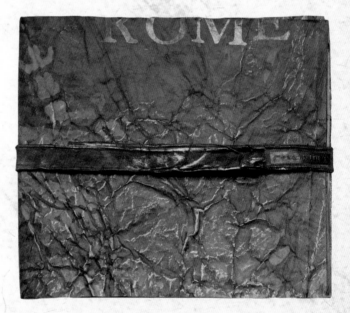

Vietnam Journal Portfolio, 1998, 16 pieces 22" × 30" (56cm × 76cm) each in a case 23" × 31" (58cm × 79cm)

If you are a visual artist who works on paper in a series, you might find a portfolio cover to be a finishing touch. When the Vietnam Journal series was acquired by the Boston Museum of Fine Arts, I made a portfolio cover to house the collection, with one of the images at 50% opacity printed on the folded cover.

Fault Lines, 2006 six folios (24 pages back and front) 8¾" × 9¼" (22cm × 24cm) each, unbound with metal binding strap

Fault Lines was created of folios cut from a single large sheet of crinkled paper painted like camouflage, sold in Rome's Piazza Navona to be used as the "ground" beneath creche displays. Reminded of Landsat photographs, I enhanced the individual pages with metallic pigment and lettering. The metal binding strap that holds them together and the title, added with a label maker, have also been colored with metallic pigment.

Adapting a Container

Collection of items

Container to hold collection

Cover image with or without text

Water-resistant drawing and painting materials of your choice

Lazertran inkjet waterslide decal

Pan of water

Glue or adhesive as needed

Glue brush

Paper towel

Solvent-based varnish, thinned with turpentine or mineral spirits

Brush, bristle

Embellishments, if desired

Optional: digital file of cover, computer, imaging software, inkjet printer, white paper for carrier sheet if needed

At a flea market, I found a vintage collection of what appeared to be British boy paper dolls with military clothing from around the world. They were designed so that you could see both the front and back of the paper soldiers. It seemed a shame to glue them to another surface, so I decided to keep them loose and find a box to house them. For the paper soldiers, a tin box, which might have been a World War I map case, seemed appropriate and was the right size.

EMPIRE

IN 1921 THE BRITISH EMPIRE CONSISTED OF
458 MILLION PEOPLE, 1/4 OF THE WORLD'S POPULATION, AND 14.2 MILLION SQUARE MILES, 1/4 OF THE EARTH'S LAND

WITH PAPER SOLDIERS PLAY "EMPIRE",
CONQUER TERRITORIES, OVERTHROW GOVERNMENTS
AND EXPLOIT RESOURCES

DOROTHY SIMPSON KRAUSE
© 2007

I decided to turn this collection into a game called "Empire" and on the cover put a world map showing the extent of the British Empire in 1921 and added the statistics that at that time 458 million people—one quarter of the world's population—were a part of the British Empire, as were 14.2 million square miles—one quarter of the Earth's land. The instructions say, "With paper soldiers play 'Empire,' conquer territories, overthrow governments and exploit resources."

1

2

3

4

1. Choose a container related to the character and size of the collection. Select a cover image or text and design the decal. Print the design face up on a Lazertran waterslide inkjet decal, following manufacturer's instructions. Let the ink dry, then place the decal in a pan of water.

2. When the decal releases from the backing paper, remove it carefully from the water. If the surface is nonporous, (such as the tin map container I am using), use the glue already on the Lazertran decal. If the surface is porous, like board or wood, coat the surface with additional glue.

3. When the decal is in the right position, pat it gently with a paper towel to help it adhere and to absorb moisture.

4. The decal goes on clear but becomes opaque white as it dries. When it is completely dry, to make it transparent again, brush on a coat of a solvent-based varnish, like Golden MSA varnish, thinned with turpentine to make it spread easily.

    As my decal became transparent, I realized that the water had caused the tin to begin to rust in spots all over the surface. It gave an impression of decay that suited the concept.

Empire, 2007, collection of paper dolls of variable sizes in tin container 9" × 4¼" × 1" (23cm × 11cm × 3cm)

Because it seemed the soldiers would be difficult to remove from the tin, I made an envelope out of a sheet of acetate and glued a piece of ribbon around the envelope lengthwise, leaving it loose as it came over the top. I printed the word "empire" onto another sheet of acetate, cut it into a strip long enough to wrap around the envelope crosswise and glued the overlapping ends together in the back. The strip adds a decorative title and also slides up and down to hold the ribbon in place.

- If you're using a hard spine liner on your drumleaf book, to allow the book to open flat, only glue the material covering the spine to the front and back covers, not to the spine of the book.

- If you have cut your recess too large for what you are embedding, or if the edges of the object are too light, color any exposed area with black marker and it will blend into the shadow.

- You can size leather to keep it from stretching and also make it soft and pliable for wrapping. Mix a small amount of wheat paste (see page 10). Coat your leather, back and front, with the wheat paste and let it rest for ½ hour. Scrape the paste out of the leather with a Teflon folder – other implements, including fingernails, can leave marks in the leather. Wrap or shape the leather while it's still damp.

- Remember to replace scrap paper under your work each time you glue to help avoid unwanted glue marks.

- Boxes and other containers can be found almost everywhere you look, some for little or no money. Begin a collection that you can choose from when you need inspiration.

- If a box doesn't seem to work as a book, think about using it to hold a book.

- Make your containers appropriate to the collections they house. Make them as important as their contents.

- In addition to inkjet printing you can draw or write on Lazertran waterslide decal with materials that are water resistant.

Viewpoint, 2007, 6" × 4½" (15cm × 11cm) closed, 6" × 36" (15cm × 91cm) open (See pages 120–121.)

- Be open to working with materials like aluminum, Plexiglas, mirror, polymer clay, ceramic and found materials.

- Try making your own bookcloth with one of the fusible heat bonding materials available in fabric stores and online. Following their directions, place a layer of your fabric, heat bonding material and archival tissue backing between sheets of parchment or Teflon and fuse them together with a medium hot iron.

- Consider texturing and painting wood covers.

- Paring leather with a knife or a machine is a useful skill to learn if you expect to work often with this material. It will enable you to remove excess thickness so that overlapping edges become invisible.

- Remember that your cover has a back as well as a front. Consider carrying your concept to both surfaces. If your front cover doesn't have a matching back, make one in a similar size, shape and color.

- Experiment with combining materials on your covers. Just remember to start with a base that won't warp with the addition of heavy items or the introduction of moisture.

- Cloth or sized leather can be stretched into shallow indentations or over thin forms to create decorative shapes or house items on your cover.

- Think about containers that suggest content: empty pill bottles, film cartridges, heart-shaped candy boxes. Each of them could be used to tell a variety of stories.

WHAT'S LEFT?

In this book, we focused on relatively simple and elegant ways to present content, but we only began to scratch the surface of all the things that are possible in the world of artist books. You will want to look at the works of many other book artists, explore innovative surfaces and unique ways of incorporating images and words, work with new media, try more complex bindings and always keep your eyes open for interesting objects that can be transformed.

My most immediate goals are to work on becoming more skillful with handling leather, to learn the barest rudiments of using a letterpress, to look at how I might adapt historical book models in contemporary ways and to become more proficient with lenticular and time-based media. I also want to begin to edition and sell my books—a large new learning curve for me.

The following pages contain a glossary of terms and resource information that you can use to explore additional options as you continue making innovative artist books, but, like this book, they are limited in scope. Join groups, search online, read books, take workshops, ask questions and gather information wherever you can. Because artist books can encompass virtually any other art form, there will always be something exciting to learn.

Man, 2006, 11½" × 10½" × 10½" (29cm × 27cm × 27cm) (6 images 6" × 4½" [15cm × 11cm] each) from the series Ars Longa

GLOSSARY

ACCORDION A long sheet of paper, folded back and forth on itself that mimics the peaks and valleys of an accordion.

ARCHIVAL Ages well with anticipated longevity.

AWL Sharpened metal rod used to punch holes.

BINDING The method and materials used to hold a book together.

BOARD Binder's board, book board, wood or other cover material.

BRAYER Roller for flattening, transferring and adhering surfaces.

BURNISH To smooth and polish a surface or help adhere it to another.

CALIPERS A hinged device that can be adjusted to the size of the object or space being measured and then either show the dimensions on a scale or dial.

CALLIGRAPHY The art of beautiful writing.

CALCIUM CARBONATE Natural compound used as whitening or thickening agent. Chalk and limestone are examples of calcium carbonate.

CHINE-COLLÉ Paper adhered to a second, often larger, piece to make a single sheet.

CHOPPING MAT Thin, lightweight, inexpensive plastic surface found in kitchen supply stores.

CODEX A book with folios sewn together with a cover.

COLD WAX MEDIUM A mixture of beeswax and spirits. Microcrystalline wax, a petroleum-based product, may also be referred to as cold wax.

COLLAGE A composition made from fragments of diverse elements glued together.

COLLAGRAPH A print with some surface texture made from a collaged plate.

COLOPHON Information on the production of the book, usually in the back.

CONCERTINA See accordion.

DAMAR A natural resin that, when dissolved in turpentine, yields a varnish, thickened stand oil or glazing medium. Also used in making encaustic medium.

DEBOSS To indent a design or lettering into a surface.

DECKLE A frame used in hand paper making, and the natural irregular edges that it produces.

DRUMLEAF BINDING A method of building a book block by joining folded pages together at the spine edge and the fore edge.

EDITION The number of copies produced of a book or other work of art. A limited edition states a fixed number that will not be exceeded.

EMBOSS To raise a design or lettering onto a surface.

ENCAUSTIC Melted beeswax medium used for painting.

EPHEMERA Printed matter not intended for preservation, frequently discarded odds and ends of printed materials.

FINE PRESS A press that makes handcrafted printed books with the highest standards of craftsmanship and attention to detail.

FOLDER Tool made from bone, plastic or Teflon, used to score, fold and smooth paper and other materials.

FOLIO A sheet of paper, or other material, folded in half to make the two-leaf, four-page unit of a book.

FOXING Stains, spots, blotches and browning in old paper.

FULL-BLEED Borderless image printed to the edges of paper or other surface.

GAFFER'S TAPE A matte black duct tape.

GESSO Paint with calcium carbonate added to give greater body and thickness. Frequently used to size canvas.

GOLD LEAF Thin sheets of gold applied to surfaces with adhesive.

GRAIN The direction in which the majority of the fibers in a piece of paper or board are aligned.

GUTTER The space formed by the two inner margins of facing pages.

HEAT PRESS Machine used primarily for transferring images. May also exert heat and pressure for pressing materials smooth or softening glue.

IMPOSITION Laying out of multiple pages for printing so that they will read consecutively when folded, cut and bound.

KERNING The space between letters, or the process of adjusting them.

LAMINATOR Roller device that adheres two items together; also used as a press to transfer images.

LEADING The spacing between lines of text.

LETTERPRESS Printing from a raised inked surface pressed on paper, resulting in lightly debossed type.

LONGSTITCH Binding that attaches the signatures directly to the spine instead of to each other with a simple in-and-out stitching; also written as long-stitch or long stitch.

MEDIA Artist materials or, in digital printing, the surface or substrate, on which the image is printed onto.

MICROSPATULA A thin flexible tool with tapered flat or rounded ends. It is useful for placing small amounts of glue or paste, scoring or reaching into tight spaces.

MONOPRINT Transfer print in which at least part of the image is made on a fixed matrix that allows repeatable prints.

MONOTYPE Paint or ink on a flat surface transferred to paper as a unique print.

MOULD A flat screen used to align an even layer of fibers to form a sheet of handmade paper. In Western papermaking, it is accompanied by a wooden frame called a deckle.

MULL A stiff, muslin-like fabric with open weave.

PARING The thinning of leather edges.

PASTILLES Small, flat balls of beeswax that melt quickly. Used in encaustic.

PASTE PAPER Paper painted with a mixture of wheat paste and acrylic paint.

PIERCING CRADLE A V-shaped device designed to hold aligned signatures while piercing holes for sewing.

PIGMENT INK For inkjet printing, offers more permanence than dye ink, but with more restricted color gamut.

PIZZA WHEELS Serrated-edged wheels that move paper through printers. If positioned after print heads, they may track through wet ink, damaging the print or printer.

POLYPROPYLENE Translucent or white plastic that almost nothing will adhere to; sold in rigid sheets 1/16" or thicker. Plastic trash bags and drop cloths are forms of flexible polypropylene.

POSTCOAT Clear liquid or spray applied as final coat to protect work.

PRECOAT In inkjet printing, a receptor coating applied to a substrate to improve color and clarity of a print and to allow water-based ink to adhere to nonporous substrates.

QUIRE Historically refers to a gathering of many leaves of parchment or paper, folded one within the other, in a manuscript or book.

REGISTRATION The alignment of an image for a particular placement.

SAFE-RELEASE TAPE A masking tape that holds and releases with no damage to the underlying paper.

SCREW PUNCH A paper drill in which the shaft rotates as you press down, cutting a clean hole.

SCORE A sharp indentation made to induce a fold.

SIGNATURE A group of folios placed one inside the other to be sewn into a book.

SIZING Material such as glue, gelatin or starch added to paper pulp or applied to the surface of paper to provide resistance to the penetration of liquid.

SPACERS Strips of paper the height of the book sewn into the spine to provide for additional materials. Sometimes referred to as guards.

SPREAD Facing pages, left and right, sometimes referred to as a double-page spread.

STAY A piece of material through which a tacket is stitched to help keep it from tearing.

STRAIGHTEDGE A long piece of heavy steel with a beveled edge. Similar to a ruler but without markings, its weight and length make it ideal to cut against.

SUBSTRATE Underlying surface for paint, print or transfer.

SWELL When the spine edge or fore edge of a book is thicker than the opposite edge.

TACKET A single stitch made with a thin strip of leather, usually through a stay.

TACKING IRON A small nonstick heat surface with a curved sole used in dry mounting, gluing collages or other tasks where the application of heat is needed.

TEMPLATE A precisely made guide, often of paper or cardboard, used to transfer a pattern.

TORTILLON A rolled stick of paper shaped to a point at one or both ends that is used to blend and smudge pencil, pastel and charcoal; also called a blending stump.

TRANSFER To move an image or text from one surface to another using various methods, including water, gel medium, Citra-solv, alcohol gel and commercially available products.

TURN-IN The extra board covering material (leather, fabric, paper), or margin, folded over the board edges.

VELLUM An untanned animal skin that has been scraped very thin and preserved with alum. Stiffer than leather, it is usually off-white.

WATERLEAF PAPER Paper made with little or no sizing.

RESOURCES

AUTHOR CONTACT

Dorothy Simpson Krause
www.dotkrause.com
dotkrause@dotkrause.com
Krause's editioned books may be purchased at:
www.viewpointeditions.com

SOURCES OF INFORMATION

The Book Arts Web
www.philobiblon.com
Information on educational opportunities, professional organizations, tutorials, reference materials and galleries. Source of The Bonefolder and the home of the Book Arts-L listserv. Maintained by Peter D.Verheyen, Syracuse University.

Wilhelm Imaging Research
www.wilhelm-research.com
Information on ink longevity.

AMIEN: Art Materials Information and Education Network
www.amien.org
A resource for artists dedicated to providing the most comprehensive, up-to-date, accurate and unbiased information about artist materials.

ART AND BOOKMAKING MATERIALS

For general and specialized art supplies not found at local dealers:

Daniel Smith
(800) 426-7923
www.danielsmith.com
Manufactures and sells a wide selection of artist materials, including digital fine-art papers.

Golden Artist Colors
(800) 959-6543
www.goldenpaints.com
Manufactures high-quality, widely distributed acrylic paints and mediums, including gel medium and digital grounds, and is an excellent source of technical information.

Talas
(212) 219-0770
www.talasonline.com
Manufactures and sells a wide selection of bookmaking supplies.

PhotoBook Creator
(800) 864-2463
www.myphotobookcreator.com
Is an inexpensive thermal adhesive binder by Unibind.

GLUES AND ADHESIVES

For finding more about glues:
www.thistothat.com
www.amazinggoop.com

MACtac
(866) 262-2822
www.mactac.com
Manufactures crystal-clear adhesive film for mounting and UGlu, an industrial-strength bonding adhesive in strips.

PAPERS

Innova Art
(856) 456-3200
www.innovaart.com
Manufactures inkjet precoated book art papers, dual sided with consistent grain direction.

Arches (Canson USA)
(800) 628-9283
www.canson-us.com
Makes widely distributed fine-art papers.

Convert-all, Inc.
(800) SYN-PAPER
www.protect-allpm.com
Makes several synthetic surfaces, including Yupo.

Twinrocker Handmade Paper
(800) 757-8946
www.twinrocker.com
Makes archival inkjet handmade papers, and carries related items.

PLASTICS

For rolled and sheet plastics not found at local hardware stores or other outlets specializing in plastics:

Regal Plastics
(800) 441-1553
www.regal-plastics.com
Sheet plastics; a minimum order of $25 and will cut and ship anywhere in the U.S.

PRECOATS AND POSTCOATS

Golden Artist Colors
(800) 959-6543
www.goldenpaints.com
Universal inkjet precoats and postcoats.

inkAid
(888) 424-8167
www.inkaid.com